101 UX PRINCIPLES

A definitive design guide

Will Grant

BIRMINGHAM - MUMBAI

101 UX Principles

Acquisition Editors: Dominic Shakeshaft, Suresh Jain
Project Editor: Radhika Atitkar
Technical Editor: Nidhisha Shetty
Proofreader: Safis Editing
Indexer: Pratik Shirodkar
Graphics: Sandip Tadge
Production Coordinator: Sandip Tadge
Photo credits: Louis Brassard

First published: December 2018

Production reference: 2211218

Published by Packt Publishing Ltd.
Livery Place
35 Livery Street
Birmingham B3 2PB, UK.
ISBN 978-1-78883-736-1
www.packtpub.com

`mapt.io`

Mapt is an online digital library that gives you full access to over 5,000 books and videos, as well as industry leading tools to help you plan your personal development and advance your career. For more information, please visit our website.

Why subscribe?

- Spend less time learning and more time coding with practical eBooks and Videos from over 4,000 industry professionals
- Learn better with Skill Plans built especially for you
- Get a free eBook or video every month
- Mapt is fully searchable
- Copy and paste, print, and bookmark content

PacktPub.com

Did you know that Packt offers eBook versions of every book published, with PDF and ePub files available? You can upgrade to the eBook version at `www.PacktPub.com` and as a print book customer, you are entitled to a discount on the eBook copy. Get in touch with us at `service@packtpub.com` for more details.

At `www.PacktPub.com`, you can also read a collection of free technical articles, sign up for a range of free newsletters, and receive exclusive discounts and offers on Packt books and eBooks.

CONTRIBUTORS

About the author

Will Grant is a British UI/UX expert and a digital product designer. He is a web technology entrepreneur with over 20 years' experience, leading teams (and products) at the intersection of technology and usability. After his Computer Science degree, Will trained with Jakob Nielsen and Bruce Tognazzini at the Nielsen Norman Group – the world leaders in usable design. Since then, Will has overseen the user experience and interaction design of several large-scale web sites and apps, reaching over a billion users in the process. Will is a "design purist" and obsessed with building beautiful, compelling, and familiar products that customers intuitively know how to use.

With thanks to Noah and Claire

About the reviewers

Billy Hollis is a designer, developer, consultant, trainer, author, speaker, and contrarian. He leads a team of world-class XAML devs at `http://nextver.com`. Billy has been developing software for over thirty years and has acquired a worldwide reputation in software development and architecture. As a developer and consultant, he has developed systems for healthcare, energy, telecommunications, and human resources. As an author, Billy has written or co-written ten technology books and dozens of magazine articles. As a conference speaker, he has spoken to thousands of software developers at major industry events, including TechEd, DevConnections, and VSLive.

Daniel Thompson is a veteran software developer and seasoned expert in delivering digital products. With over 20 years' experience in the systems design, architecture, stability, and scaling of both business and consumer software, Daniel has a proven track record of delivering powerful, rock solid products for global corporations.

In his work with start-ups, Daniel has helped countless teams take their initial idea through to a minimum viable product that solves customer needs and is ready to scale. He is also the founder of D4 Software—the makers of Prodlytic, SQLizer, and QueryTree.

Kate Shaw is a freelancer and the Head of product design. She is a communicator, creator, problem solver, travel maven, freelance thinker, Wannabe revolutionary, and a mum, with fifteen years' experience of creating delightful digital experiences. Kate is articulate and professional with a passion for a user-centric design.

Balancing commercial and people's needs, Kate designs people-intuitive experiences for start-ups, FTSE 100 companies, and agencies. Her clients have included BBC, The Telegraph, The Guardian, John Lewis, Marks & Spencers, Hotels.com, Digitas, Ogilvy, and Yoti.

Packt is Searching for Authors Like You

If you're interested in becoming an author for Packt, please visit authors.packtpub.com and apply today. We have worked with thousands of developers and tech professionals, just like you, to help them share their insight with the global tech community. You can make a general application, apply for a specific hot topic that we are recruiting an author for, or submit your own idea.

TABLE OF CONTENTS

PREFACE

These 101 principles are a broad set of guidelines for designing digital products. There are no doubt thousands more, but these are the core principles that will make most products more usable and effective. They'll save you time and make users happier.

Somewhere along the journey of the web maturing, we forgot something important: user experience is not art. It's the opposite of art. UX design should perform a function: serving users. It has to still *look* great, but not at the expense of *actually working*. Poor design has crept in over the years and some digital products have become worse in 100 tiny ways.

So how did we get here? Branding agencies got involved. They insisted that because as a company we always refer to photos as "memories," the photo menu should be called memories too. Nobody knows what it means or how to find their photos.

The CEO *personally* picked the shade of sea breeze that the company uses for its headings everywhere, so all the headings are pale blue. This means nobody can read them against a white background on their mobile phone screen.

The marketing department decided that a full-screen pop-up collecting users' email addresses would be good for the Quarter 4 CRM metrics. Then they said, "Oh, don't make the close icon too big because we don't want customers to actually close it."

In these three simple examples, found all over the web, the company lost sight of the user's needs and forgot to put the user first. Over the past 20 years, I've learned a lot about designing digital products. It's hard to pick all these individual lessons out because it feels like they've been compiled into a big UX operating system in my brain.

I'm not ashamed to admit that I'm a design purist. Of course, I value aesthetics, but I see them as a "hygiene factor" and a necessity. Beyond the veneer of aesthetics, I've always strived to produce software that's usable and powerful, where the features are instantly obvious or easy to discover and learn.

This book is a "shortcut to success" for less experienced designers and a challenge to some accepted thinking for seasoned UX professionals.

The principles are structured into broad sections such as typography, controls, journeys, consistency, and the wider field of UX practice. Feel free to dip in and out and use the book as a reference, although it has been designed to be read through in order, if you wish.

You might find yourself disagreeing with some of the principles—that's fine because this is, after all, an opinionated book—but the disagreement will sometimes be a prompt to examine your accepted thinking and re-evaluate if there might be a better way to accomplish your users' goals.

I hope you enjoy the book and that it helps you to become a better UX professional, so that you can implement experiences that work, avoid common pitfalls, and grow your confidence to fight for the user.

Will Grant, August 2018

#01

ANYONE CAN BE
A USER EXPERIENCE
(UX) PROFESSIONAL

This guide is for anyone who designs software products as part of their work. You may be a full-time designer, a UX professional or someone who has to make decisions about UX in your organization's products. Regardless of your role, the principles in this guide will improve your products, help you to serve your users' needs better, and make your customers more likely to return to you.

Although various examples throughout this book feature a mobile app, website, web app, or some desktop software, the principles are applicable to a wide range of applications, from in-car UI, mobile games, and cockpit controls, to washing machine interfaces and everything in between.

Empathy and objectivity are the primary skills you must possess to be good at UX. This is not to undermine those who have spent many years studying and working in the UX field—their insights and experience are valuable—rather to say that study and practice alone are not enough.

You need empathy to understand your users' needs, goals and frustrations. You need objectivity to look at your product with fresh eyes, spot the flaws and fix them. You can learn everything else.

Learning points

- UX isn't a talent you're born with—you can learn how to be good in this field
- Objectivity and empathy are the two key personality traits you need to display
- This book aims to provide a shortcut to success with 101 tried-and-tested principles

#02

DON'T USE MORE THAN TWO TYPEFACES

Only amateurs call typefaces "fonts", you know? "Proper" design professionals call them "typefaces." Fonts are the files on the device that the software *uses* to render the typeface. Fonts are the paint on the palette, while the typeface is the masterpiece on the canvas.

Regardless, too often designers add too many typefaces to their products. You should aim to use two typefaces maximum: one for headings and titles, and another for body copy that is intended to be read.

Use weights and italics *within* that font family for emphasis—rather than switching to another family. Typically, this means using your corporate brand font as the heading, while leaving the controls, dialogs and in-app copy (which need to be clearly legible) in a more proven, readable typeface.

Using too many typefaces creates too much visual "noise" and increases the effort that the user has to put into understanding the view in front of them. What's more, many custom-designed brand typefaces are often made with punchy visual impact in mind, not readability.

Learning points

- Use two typefaces maximum
- Use one typeface for headings and titles
- Use another typeface for body copy

#03

USERS ALREADY HAVE FONTS ON THEIR COMPUTERS, SO USE THEM

Yes, your corporate brand font is lovely. It's so playful and charming but it takes an extra three seconds to load the page, as the font needs to be downloaded from the server and rendered—and nothing appears until it loads—driving your users crazy.

Including custom display fonts for headings and titles is fine; it helps to brand the product and adds some visual interest. However, using custom fonts for body copy is generally a bad idea.

First of all, these fonts have to be loaded from somewhere, whether it's Google Fonts, Typekit or your own CDN. This means that there is an overhead in getting the font files down to the user's machine. Content-heavy pages will often break while the correct fonts are downloaded and rendered—the dreaded **Flash of unstyled content** or **Flash of unstyled text** (FOUC) (https://en.wikipedia.org/wiki/Flash_of_unstyled_content).

Secondly, if, by specifying wild and wonderful body copy typefaces, you think you're exerting some control over the end result, then think again: responsive design and 1,000s of different devices out in the wild mean your pages will look a little different for everyone.

Luckily, whether your user is on a phone or a desktop, Windows or Mac (or Linux), they have some beautiful, highly-readable fonts already installed and waiting to be used. The "system font stack" is a CSS rule that tells modern browsers to render type in the system-native typeface.

In most cases, using system-native fonts makes pages appear more quickly, and the type look sharper and more readable.

```
Font-family:
    apple-system
    BlinkMacSystemFont
    Segoe UI
    Roboto
    Oxygen-Sans
    Ubuntu
    Cantarell
    Helvetica Neue
    sans-serif
```

Please, just use the system font stack.

Learning points

- Use the system-native fonts that your users already have installed
- System fonts will typically render better than custom ones
- Using native fonts speeds up page load time

#04

USE TYPE SIZE TO DEPICT INFORMATION HIERARCHY

This is a simple, but effective, method for organizing your views and making them instantly understandable for a wide range of users. Let's look at an example of how not to do this in an imagined "Calendar" app user interface:

Simply by altering the type size by a noticeable factor, we can show the user the most relevant information first:

Scale up the information that you want users to see first, or that you think they'll find most useful, and they can read on further for extra detail. This is the reason for a lot of news and factual journalism settling on this format:

Headline that tells you something

Subtitle that adds context and poses more questions

This is body copy that expands on the story by adding detail progressively through the copy. Keep reading to the end to learn less and less important detail.

The exact same technique can be employed in user interface design to great effect.

Design blog 'A List Apart' uses typographic hierarchy
to excellent effect on its article list

[**Pro-tip**: Find a balance and don't overdo it. If too many elements on the page are large, then they lose any sense of hierarchy and emphasis.]

Learning points

- Type size indicates the importance of information to users

- Use at least two, but no more than three, type sizes

- Think about which bits of information are most important to your users

#05

USE A SENSIBLE DEFAULT SIZE FOR BODY COPY

Your customers will be reading a lot of text across your app or site, so how big should the type be?

The days of fixed-size type are long gone. Most browsers on desktop and mobile will let users scale type up and down, switch into "reading mode" and apply system-wide accessibility settings, like large type and high-contrast colors.

With that in mind, all you're doing here is setting the *default* type size that appears when the product is first opened. Ideally, the type should be big enough to be readable, but not so big as to overwhelm the user or take up too much space in a crowded view.

Body copy in 16px, with a 1.5 line height and "auto" or "default" character spacing, is usually a safe bet and a good default for the vast majority of your users.

Trying to set your own character spacing is usually unnecessary for body copy, because the browser will do a better job of text rendering than you can.

Learning points

- Body copy in 16px, with a 1.5 line height and "auto" or "default" character spacing, is the "gold standard" for readable text
- Allow users to scale your type up and down for their device
- Don't ever disable device-scaling features

#06

USE AN ELLIPSIS
TO INDICATE THAT
THERE'S A FURTHER STEP

If your user sees a "Remove" button, how do they know if pressing it will:

- Remove the "thing" they're looking at?

- Ask which "thing" needs to be removed?

- Ask them if they really want to remove the "thing"?

- Instantly remove all their stuff?

Label the button "Remove…" and the user will have a good idea that there's another step before all their stuff is removed. Most users will infer from this that the button is the first part of a multi-part process and there will be a second step to confirm or cancel the action. If a control requires an extra step to perform its action, include an ellipsis (…) in the control:

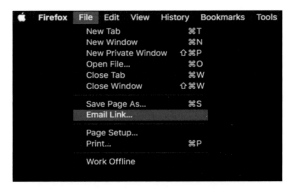

New Tab just opens a new tab, while **Email Link…** will ask for more information in the next step

These little dots are a great example of invisible design: most users will never have even noticed them, but they impart a subtle message as a user's experience builds over time. They don't get in the way and they "just work."

Learning points

- If the user needs to perform an additional action, show an ellipsis
- An ellipsis can give the user more confidence that there's a further step to confirm an action
- Users may well have unconsciously learned what these dots mean in a **User Interface (UI)**

#07

MAKE YOUR BUTTONS LOOK LIKE BUTTONS

The flat design aesthetic, born out of Microsoft's Metro user interface, rose to near ubiquity in the late 2000s. In iOS 7 and Android's material design, these extremely minimal visuals are still the go-to look for modern web applications.

Flat design is bad. It's really terrible for usability. It's style over substance and it forces your users to think more about every interaction they make with your product. Stop making it hard for your customers to find the buttons:

The Metro user interface in all its "what is clickable?" splendor

There are parts of your UI that can be interacted with, but your user neither knows which parts these are, nor wants to spend time learning this. They have used buttons in real life, many times—on elevator controls, on their oven, and in their car—so they understand how a button works:

Buttons that exhibit visual affordances such as texture and pseudo-3D shadows (left) consistently perform better in user tests than those without them (right)

By drawing on real-world examples, we can make UI buttons that are obvious and instantly familiar. The human visual system is tuned to see depth, and by removing the illusion of depth from your UI, you remove a whole layer of information for the user.

Buttons in real life look pushable: they're raised or they suggest an obvious way that they might move if pushed. For example, they might have an indicator light and look more prominent when enabled. You should copy these features into your UI.

The inverse is also true: there are real-world buttons that *don't* look pushable—flat capacitive buttons on car park machines and coffee machines spring to mind—and these buttons are often accompanied by a stuck-on, handwritten *press here for ticket* note.

Using real-life inspiration to create affordances, a new user can identify the controls right away. Create the visual cues your user needs to know instantly that they're looking at a button that can be tapped or clicked:

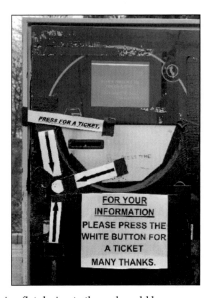

Bringing flat design to the real world has consequences

Lastly, the opposite is also true: don't make non-button elements look like buttons if they're not.

Learning points

- Make buttons look like buttons
- Don't make non-buttons look like buttons
- Borrow ideas from real-world experiences in your UI

#08

MAKE BUTTONS
A SENSIBLE SIZE
AND GROUP THEM
TOGETHER BY FUNCTION

The US psychologist Paul Fitts wrote a paper in 1954 called The information capacity of the human motor system in controlling the amplitude of movement (https://www.ncbi.nlm.nih.gov/pubmed/13174710) which was published in the *Journal of Experimental Psychology*. Fitts' work would go on to be one of the most well-studied models of human motion.

To dumb Fitts' Law down for us UX people, rather than psychologists, the core concept that applies to us is:

> **"The time required to rapidly move to a target area is a function of the ratio between the distance to the target and the size of the target."**

If you're building a user interface, it's really simple to do this: make buttons big enough, and close enough, that users can efficiently find them and move between them:

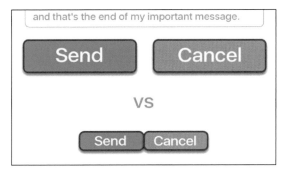

Which is easier to use and less error-prone?

A great anti-pattern example is those tiny "x" buttons to close pop-up ads: it's almost as if the advertisers don't want you to close them...

Learning points

- Make buttons big enough that they can be tapped or clicked easily
- Place buttons close enough to be reachable
- Don't cause "misclicks" by placing buttons too close together

#09

**MAKE THE WHOLE
BUTTON CLICKABLE,
NOT JUST THE TEXT**

Maybe this is simply a pet hate of mine, but I see it often enough to mention it here. Buttons often feature text and sometimes developers *only make the text clickable*, not the whole button. Meaning that, if you're a couple of pixels out and miss the text (but hit the button)... nothing happens.

We're all familiar with thinking, "Did I not click that?" and often this is the cause. If you're imitating the real-world behavior of a button, then make it behave like a real button. This includes giving the user some feedback that the button has been successfully clicked (or tapped). This could be with a change of shade, a slight 1-pixel-movement "down" or a subtle audio effect.

You get bonus points for showing the "hand pointer" to desktop users. Sloppy programming means that some web apps don't show this and it's unforgivable.

Learning points

- Your button should look and behave like a button—clicking anywhere on the button should activate it
- Make the pointer turn into a hand when you hover over the button on desktop
- Give the user some visual feedback that the button has been clicked

#10

DON'T INVENT NEW, ARBITRARY CONTROLS

This could be:

- An isometric pseudo-3D wheel to choose the color of your car

- A volume dial that you must click and drag up-and-down to "rotate"

- A button you must click and hold for a few seconds to indicate that you *really* want to do this action

Just don't invent them. As designers, we already have a rich palette of existing controls to choose from. If you're thinking about making a new UI control, please stop and think about how hard it will be for users to learn yet another interface pattern. I promise you this—there's already a way to do what you want to do.

However, every now and then, something new comes along that is genuinely an advance in UI. Back in 2008, Loren Brichter made a Twitter app called **Tweetie**, with a unique pull-to-refresh interaction. Pulling the view down would show "release to refresh" and releasing would show a spinner. The pull-to-refresh interaction went on to be included in Twitter, which bought Tweetie, and then in iOS and Android apps in their hundreds.

So, don't invent new controls... unless they're astonishingly good.

Learning points

- Don't invent your own UI
- There's almost certainly a UI component out there that does what you need
- Don't make users learn your new thing

#11

SEARCH SHOULD BE A TEXT FIELD WITH A BUTTON LABELED "SEARCH"

Search has, over the years, been over-designed. One common anti-pattern is hiding search behind a control to activate it. Slowing the user down and adding an extra step might remove an input field from your view but at the expense of familiarity.

If you're offering your users a search function, then show them a text field with a search button. If you're using an icon, then use a "magnifying glass" icon. This is the archetype and using anything else makes no sense anymore.

The "gold standard"

On a mobile phone screen, there may not be enough space to always show the search field, but I'd still encourage you to evaluate if you can. Tucking the search field into the top of a scrolling view can work well:

Search at the top of a list view that only appears when "pulled down"

Bonus points: when the user taps the **Search** tab in a mobile app, show the search view, move the cursor to the search field and show the device keyboard for them.

Learning points

- Search should be a text field with a search button
- Only use the "magnifying glass" icon for search
- Move the focus to the search field when the **Search** tab is tapped on mobile

#12

SLIDERS SHOULD
BE USED ONLY FOR
NON-QUANTIFIABLE
VALUES

Designer: "Oh, cool, this UI kit has a nice-looking slider; let's use it for everything!"

User (trying to set a value): *smashes up phone*

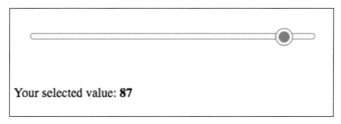

I was trying to select 86

If you've ever fiddled with a tiny touchscreen, while trying to set a value with a slider, you'll be familiar with the preceding scenario. Even on a desktop screen with a mouse, it's a pain in the ass.

Slider controls should never be used for setting specific numeric values. They are, however, great for volume controls, brightness and color mix values, where the slider can be used to pick a qualitative value and the actual numeric value itself doesn't matter.

For precise numbers, refer to *#13, Use Numeric Entry Fields For Precise Integers.*

Learning points

- Slider controls should never be used for setting specific numeric values

- Use sliders for adjusting qualitative settings like volume and brightness

- Make the slider control a sensible size that can be easily grabbed by the user's pointing device

#13

USE NUMERIC ENTRY FIELDS FOR PRECISE INTEGERS

If you're trying to get an integer (a whole number) from a user—for example the number of widgets they want to order or the number of days an event runs for—it makes no sense to offer them a free text input field where they can enter "a few" or " 👻 ." A numeric entry field in HTML is:

```
<input type="number">
```

This will display slightly differently on different devices and that's the whole point. By adapting to the control system of the client's device, the user gets simpler entry and makes fewer mistakes. You also get fewer emoji in your database.

Of course, a huge benefit here is that this will improve your form conversion rates, by giving users on both desktop and mobile a quick, painless way to enter numbers into forms. Users abandon forms because they're too long, ask for too many details or because it's difficult to enter information into the form.

Learning points

- Numeric input controls should be used for setting specific numeric values
- Let the browser or device determine the best input method; don't "build your own" numeric entry control
- Forms always require more effort from users than just consuming content, so minimize the amount of "things" you ask them for

#14

**DON'T USE A
DROP-DOWN MENU
IF YOU ONLY HAVE
A FEW OPTIONS**

A drop-down menu in the user interface is designed to expand when clicked and present a range of options. This is fine for country selection or customization, where there *genuinely are* lots of options.

There is, however, an overhead to operating a drop-down menu: the user needs to click to open, scroll to the correct item, then click to select. On a mobile device this can be even slower, as the user will be using a smaller screen.

If you only have two or three options, then don't jump to using a drop-down straightaway. Consider whether the options could be better presented to users with a different kind of control (radio buttons, sliders, and so on).

Sort your options into a sensible order— alphabetical or numerical—rather than random. Don't be the app that asks users to select a floor of a building in alphabetical order: "First, Fourth, Ground, Second, Third." Yes, I've seen this!

Very long drop-downs—for example, country selection—can benefit from a mini search or filter control: begin typing "U" and only see "Ukraine, United Arab Emirates, United Kingdom" and so on. This allows your user to skip to the section they need.

Mobile users actually have a head start here: most mobile operating systems will show a full-width "picker" control for drop-down selection, which is much less fiddly to use on a small touchscreen:

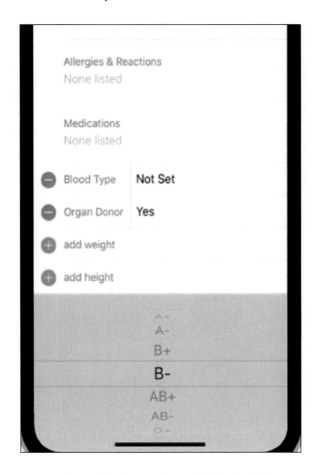

Picking a blood type with a mobile "picker" UI

Learning points:

- Drop-down menus can be a pain, so only use them if you need to

- Offer the ability to search in very long drop-downs

- Drop-downs can be useful in mobile apps, as the user will have a specialized UI to use

#15

ALLOW USERS TO
UNDO DESTRUCTIVE
ACTIONS

The *ohnosecond* (https://en.oxforddictionaries. com/definition/ohnosecond) is the split second when you realize you've made a terrible mistake. Your stomach sinks, your trembling hands lift from the keyboard and you freeze. This moment of horror could be deleting a customer's records, emailing what you really think of your boss directly to your boss, or hitting "buy now" on 111 items, when you really wanted one.

The best apps allow users to back out of such actions, either with undo controls or by giving users the ability to edit actions before they're final. Google's Gmail has had an optional "undo send" feature for quite some time. This stores your sent message in a "buffer" for 20 seconds, giving you that short grace period to cancel sending. If you just ignore it, you know the message will be sent shortly. This particular feature has saved me many times.

Users will feel more in control of your product because knowing they can undo every action and recover from mistakes will free them to experiment more with the product and hopefully get more from it.

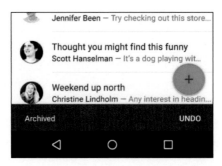

A toast-style notification with an optional "undo" control

From a UI perspective, a nice pattern is to include the **UNDO** control on a banner (or toast) that appears after an action. The user is informed that their action worked, they see a recap of what the action was, and they're given a quick shortcut to reverse that action.

Be forgiving because people make hundreds of mistakes every day and your users will love you if your product saves their ass just once.

Learning points

- Allow users to undo their mistakes
- Give users a greater sense of freedom and control
- Be forgiving—people will make mistakes

#16

THINK ABOUT WHAT'S JUST OFF THE SCREEN

Of course, we're mostly concerned with things that are on the screen, but there are also things you can hint at that aren't on the screen.

The screen is the user's viewport into your app and it forms a mental model of how they see your interface. By showing the edges of items, it's possible to show the user that there's more to be seen just off the screen.

This technique, when used well, can provide a subtle visual cue to the user that there are more items to be found, while at the same time not taking up too much screen space.

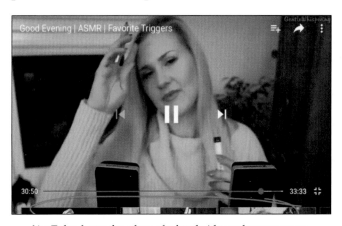

YouTube shows the edges of related videos when you pause

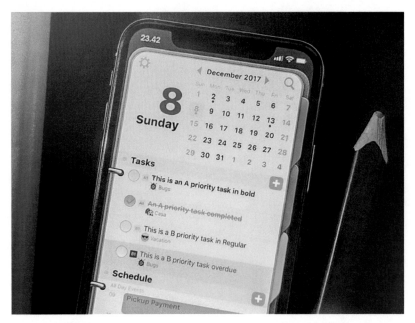

The Opus One app shows calendar dividers to indicate that there are other sections

In both of these examples, this isn't the *only* way to get to these other sections—there's a related video view in YouTube already—but it does provide a nice hint for new users and a shortcut for experienced ones.

Learning points

- Showing the edges of items that are just off screen is a good visual cue for users
- This shouldn't be the only way to navigate, but should act as a hint
- This design pattern is very efficient in terms of screen space

#17

USE "INFINITE SCROLL" FOR FEED-STYLE CONTENT ONLY

Infinite scroll—where the page just keeps scrolling, loading more items asynchronously as the user hits the bottom—is extremely handy for users.

Scrolling with a mouse wheel or a touchscreen is inherently quicker, and simpler, than clicking through pages, and when the content is a news feed of Instagram photos or Tweets, it's perfect:

Loading the next few items. I hope

However, infinite scroll should be limited to only a few types of content. If applied to finite lists (messages, emails, to-do items, and so on) then the user has no way of determining a beginning, middle, and end to the content. When used with this kind of content, infinite scroll is confusing and slower to use, so save it for feeds.

Although feeds used to be predominantly chronological—with the newest items first—more products (Facebook and Twitter, for example) are opting to offer users "algorithmically sorted" or "smart" timelines. The idea is (I assume) to offer users more relevant tweets or news stories at the top of their feed, and to allow promoted content like ads and sponsored posts to appear more prominently.

It may be personal taste, but I really dislike these smart timelines. First of all, they aim to serve companies and advertisers over the user, but, secondly, there is a real discoverability problem: you can't be sure what you're going to see when you open the timeline. Is it the latest item? Is it the most relevant? What happens when you navigate away and come back? Often, you're shown a new, regenerated list, making it impossible to find the item you just saw and thought you could come back to (see *#19, If You Must Use Infinite Scroll, Store The User's Position And Return To It*).

Whether smart or normal, infinite scroll pages have a couple of other, often overlooked, problems. They "break" the scroll bar: the scroll position on the browser window is no longer accurate and it can no longer be used to navigate up and down the page. Lastly, page footers become impossible to reach. Bear that in mind.

Learning points

- Use pagination for long lists of items
- Use infinite scroll for news-feed-style content only
- Remember the user's position if they navigate away from the feed

#18

IF YOUR CONTENT HAS A BEGINNING, MIDDLE, AND END, USE PAGINATION

Continuing from *#17, Use "Infinite Scroll" For Feed–Style Content Only* a paginated, multi-page list may seem "old school" but it has a few major benefits:

- It's goal-oriented, so the user is trying to find the item they need in a list and pagination feels intuitive, instead of that they are searching through an endless list
- It remembers the user's position and displays the current page to them
- It conveys a beginning, middle and end to the content
- Users can use the scroll bar to navigate the page and they can reach the footer if they need to

If the user sees that there are "9,999 pages", then they can make the choice to use a search, sort, or filter control. They can't make that choice if they have no idea how many pages there may be:

A great paginator

Show the user the current page, some pages before and after it, and the lowest and highest pages in the range. Adding "next" and "previous" buttons feels unnecessary.

Given all of this, users won't find it easy to search through very long lists: it's just too cognitively arduous. A search, sort or filter control should be considered mandatory on lists of more than a few pages.

Learning points

- Use pagination when the content is finite
- Show the user the current page, nearby pages and the highest and lowest pages in the range
- Offer the user search, sort, and filter controls

#19

IF YOU MUST USE
INFINITE SCROLL,
STORE THE USER'S
POSITION AND
RETURN TO IT

Often, a user will leave your infinite-scroll feed to take an action: maybe to favorite an item or post a comment. From there, they'll hit back (on desktop), swipe back (iOS) or use the hardware back button (Android).

Q: Where do they end up?

a. Right back at the top of the infinite-scroll feed again

b. Exactly where they left off

The answer is obviously b), unless you **really** hate your users. Sadly, a) is often the case on ecommerce sites, when browsing a long list of products.

Although the technical implementation details can be challenging, it's worth putting in the effort to avoid disorientating users. Viewing a product then navigating back should always return the user to the point where they left off.

Learning points

- Remember the user's position when they navigate away from long lists
- Return the user to the same point in the list or the same page in the paginator
- Don't disorientate your user unnecessarily

#20

MAKE "BLANK SLATES" MORE THAN JUST EMPTY VIEWS

A blank slate is a view that would normally show a lot of information to a user—a list of projects, albums, tasks, and so on—but because the user is new, they haven't yet created anything.

The default behavior of many apps is to simply show an empty view where the content would be. For a new user, this is a pretty poor experience and a massive missed opportunity for you to give them some extra orientation and guidance.

A blank slate is usually some helpful text, hints and maybe a friendly graphic or icon. Now, because these views can appear on a per-feature basis, it's easy to be very task-oriented in the advice you give. If the user views the to-do list, you can give advice on making the first to-do item.

On a profile, you can give the user guidance to include a bio or add an avatar picture.

The Basecamp to-do list before the user has created any items

Shopify welcomes new users with a recap of what they can do

The blank slate is only shown once (before the user has generated any content), so it's an ideal way of orienting people to the functions of your product, while getting out of the way of more established users who will hopefully "know the ropes" a little better. For that reason, it should be considered mandatory for UX designers to offer users a useful blank slate.

Learning points

- Use blank slates to orient new users
- Be task-oriented in the advice you give to users
- Be specific in your advice if you offer blank slates on a per-feature basis

#21

MAKE "GETTING STARTED" TIPS EASILY DISMISSABLE

A blank slate (refer to *#20, Make "Blank Slates" More Than Just Empty Views*) won't show once the user adds some content or performs an initial task, which is ideal.

Too often, apps force users to view their "getting started" guide or "tips for beginners." They are often good for new users, but if you're coming back to an app you've used before then they're incredibly frustrating.

An extra level of rage is induced when an app update "resets" these tips and existing users are forced to sit through the tutorial all over again just to use the app. Make tips optional and dismissable. You'll get bonus points for letting users exit the entire "onboarding wizard" with one tap:

Tell users what you're about to tell them before you actually tell them

However, beware of overdoing these tips: if you've followed conventions (and basically, the rest of this book), there shouldn't be a need to explain every little detail of your app's UI.

If you have designed and delivered a UI where you have to explain "You can search for things here," and "Your past entries appear here," and "Click here to create a new entry," then your UI is too complicated and needs to change.

Learning points

- Let users easily leave onboarding wizards
- Allow the whole tutorial to be skipped in one action
- Resist explaining too much about your UI

#22

WHEN A USER REFRESHES A FEED, MOVE THEM TO THE LAST UNREAD ITEM

Typically, a feed (or any list of items) will have links *on each item* to view them or perform actions on them. This means that users may well be navigating back and forth to these lists.

Imagine a list of news items; it's likely that a user would read the list, then choose one or more news items to read, each time navigating back to the list view. Don't simply reload the feed and put the user back to the start again, you monster!

Twitter shows the user how many "tweets" behind they are, allowing them to manually reload if they wish, but not altering the feed without their explicit action:

Twitter getting something right for a change

Of course, *technically*, the feed may well have changed in the time it took the user to read the story, but if it keeps updating, it's disorienting and difficult to use. Yes, this means additionally keeping track of where your user's scroll position is, but it's worth it for the usability benefit.

Learning points

- Return users to the same place that they came from
- Don't reload or refresh feeds while a user is using them
- Give the user an option to manually refresh the feed while they're using it

#23

DON'T HIDE
ITEMS AWAY IN A
"HAMBURGER" MENU

Few UI patterns can be as controversial as the hamburger menu. Over the past five years, it's become the de facto way of offering a menu on small displays, typically as a website scales into mobile or tablet width using responsive design:

The dreaded hamburger

Research shows ("Hamburger Menus and Hidden Navigation Hurt UX Metrics" NNG, (https://www.nngroup.com/articles/hamburger-menus/) 2016) that hamburger menus:

- Slow down discovery time for users
- Increase perceived task difficulty
- Slow down time to complete a task

Simply put, the hamburger menu hides items away from users and makes them less discoverable. Additionally, because the menu is hidden, users can't gain a sense of "where they are" in the product.

Some alternative design patterns to the hamburger menu:

- **Navigation on the bottom of the view**: Made popular by iOS apps, you can get four or five key features into an ever-present bottom menu and maybe make the fifth item "fly out" with advanced tools.

- **Tabbed navigation**: Inverting the above, and popularized by Android apps, items can live at the top of the view.

- **Vertical type:** Pin your navigation to the left of the view and orient the type vertically. It won't solve every problem, but if you have fewer than six or seven items, it's better than the hamburger.

In some circumstances, for example if your app has a lot of features that need to be "possible" (see *#96, Decide Whether an Interaction Should Be Obvious, Easy, or Possible*), the usability trade-off seems worth making, in order to offer these features on mobile rather than removing them, but never use a hamburger menu on the desktop.

If you **must** use a hamburger menu, then label it **menu** and spare the user the much-maligned "three lines" icon.

Learning points

- The hamburger menu slows down discovery for users
- By hiding menu controls in this way, users can't get a sense of their location
- Consider alternatives to the hamburger menu, but if you must use one, label it

#24

MAKE YOUR LINKS
LOOK LIKE LINKS

Links, or *hyperlinks*, are the basis of the web and were one of the key advances when Sir Tim Berners-Lee invented HTML in 1989. In the original browsers, clickable links were blue, italic, and underlined. They looked gaudy and out of place, but that was the point: it was a brand new concept and users needed a way of telling a link apart from the rest of the text on the page.

Fast-forward to the present day and the practice of styling links has largely been abandoned in favor of only highlighting them when they're hovered over or, worse, adding no visual affordances to them whatsoever.

The style-on-hover approach is less than ideal: users on touchscreen devices have no hover state. Meanwhile users with a mouse end up "hunting" for links by hovering over parts of text bit by bit, hoping to find a link, or just never finding them at all.

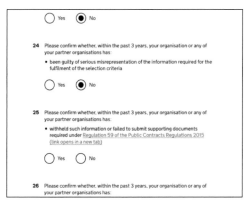

A gov.uk page with clear links and nice controls

Asking the user to click things just to work out what they do (or whether they do anything at all) is insane. This kind of design decision is a classic example of form over function. If you're making your users guess what links do, because you think that "minimalism" means adding so few affordances that controls are impossible to use, then you're wrong. I don't care what the marketing guys say: make your links underlined.

Learning points

- Make links look like links with visual affordances
- Don't make non-links look like links
- Don't make your users hunt for clickable controls

#25

SPLIT MENU
ITEMS DOWN
INTO SUBSECTIONS,
SO USERS DON'T
HAVE TO REMEMBER
LARGE LISTS

Humans are better at some things than others. We're really good, for example, at drawing a pretty picture of a flower, but we're not so good at instantly recalling the precise genus of that flower and its scientific name. Computers are better at that kind of thing.

The rule of thumb for the number of items that a person can reasonably remember and juggle in a list, is "seven, plus or minus two." (The Magical Number Seven, Plus or Minus Two: Some Limits on our Capacity for Processing Information, George A. Miller (1956) (https://www.ncbi.nlm.nih.gov/pubmed/13310704)). This research has been around since the 1950s and has been revised and re-evaluated many times over the years. I'll spare you the psychological study details, but the short version is: it's pretty much true.

The "magic number seven" will change depending on the items being recalled, the context, and environmental factors like state of mind, but it's as good a starting point as any. The point is: users can't manipulate and recall long lists of items in their minds.

Cooking & Dining	Sports & Outdoor Shoes
Furniture	Fitness
Bedding & Linens	Camping & Hiking
Home Accessories	Cycling
Arts, Crafts & Sewing	Sports Technology
Garden & Outdoors	Water Sports
All Home & Garden	Winter Sports
Garden Furniture assembly	Golf
Home Furniture assembly	Running
Wedding List	Sports Nutrition
Power, Garden & Hand Tools	All Sports & Outdoors
Kitchen & Bathroom Fixtures	Equipment Assembly
Trade & Professional Tools	Grocery
Smart Home	Beer, Wine & Spirits
Lighting	Luxury Food & Drink
All DIY & Tools	Luxury Beauty
Smart Home Services	Health & Personal Care
Pet Supplies	Diet & Nutrition
Toys & Games	Men's Grooming
Baby	Car Accessories & Parts
Kids' & Baby Fashion	Tools & Equipment
Baby Wish List	Sat Nav & Car Electronics
Jewellery	Motorbike Accessories & Parts
Watches	All Business, Industry & Science
Bags	Lab Supplies

How *not* to present users with the categories of your store

If you're presenting a user with a list of options, keep in mind that by the time they've read the seventh or eighth option, they will likely have "filled the buffer" in their mind to capacity, and will struggle to remember what the first option was.

This also applies to menus, as well as sections and categories. All of these tasks are better served by other UI patterns described elsewhere in this book.

Try to group menus into sections, or reduce the complexity of options, so that the user doesn't have to struggle to recall them. Hide extra settings in "advanced" settings, for example. Your users are (probably) humans, not robots.

Learning points

- Users can read, manipulate and recall *roughly* seven items in a list
- After more than seven or so items, the user will struggle to use the list
- Group similar items into sections

#26

HIDE "ADVANCED" SETTINGS FROM MOST USERS

There's no need to include every possible menu option in your menu when you can hide advanced settings away. Group settings together, but separate out the more obscure into their own section of "power user" settings, which should be also grouped into sections if there are a lot of them (don't just throw all the advanced items in at random).

Not only does hiding advanced settings have the effect of reducing the number of items for a user to mentally juggle (refer to *#25, Split Menu Items Down into Subsections, so Users Don't Have to Remember Large Lists*), it also makes the app appear less daunting, by hiding complex settings from most users.

By picking good defaults (refer to *#92, Pick Good Defaults*), you can ensure that the vast majority of users will never need to alter advanced settings. For the ones that do, an advanced menu section is a pretty well-used pattern.

The macOS system preferences panel is well categorized

Settings pages should be structured based on "jobs to be done", not necessarily on system function. For example, all the settings for "sound" are in one place and "video" in another. This seems obvious and many operating systems get this right, but many software products don't, instead throwing all the settings into one long settings menu, which is too dense and long to work with.

The macOS system preferences panel (in the preceding image) does this well by sorting items by conceptual area, rather than system function. **Keyboard**, **Mouse,** and **Trackpad** all have their own views, instead of calling them "Input" and lumping them together into one confusing view.

Although there are a lot of items, iOS groups them into sections

You get bonus points for putting a "search" field on particularly long or complex settings views.

Learning points

- Hide advanced settings behind another level of navigation
- Group items together by jobs to be done or conceptual area
- Remember the "seven plus or minus two" rule for long lists of items

#27

REPEAT MENU ITEMS IN THE FOOTER OR LOWER DOWN IN THE VIEW

Your site's navigation is at the top of the view, but the user has scrolled right down the view—no doubt captivated by the wonderful, engaging content you've provided—so how do they return to the top of the page?

Most mobile browsers have a shortcut where tapping the top bar of the app will scroll the page up. There's no need to provide a "back to top" link that floats down the page: it's a waste of space.

A great solution is to repeat main menu items in the footer of the page or, at the very least, add some shortcuts to popular parts of the site. Including a "mini breadcrumb" is more useful than a "back to top" link, as the user can hop back up a level to find the next item.

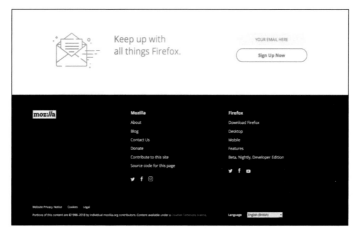

Mozilla's footer

Mozilla's footer (above) strikes a nice balance between not being overly cluttered and providing useful links to top-level sections of its navigation hierarchy. Some sites decide to include a search control in the footer, which can be a smart idea: the user may not have found what they were looking for on the page, so this gives them a way to search the site.

Learning points

- Repeat navigation items in the footer
- Don't make footers a "dead end"
- Consider offering a search function in the footer if it makes sense to do so

#28

USE CONSISTENT ICONS ACROSS THE PRODUCT

A UI packed with seemingly random, disparate icons is a usability disaster. I know what happened: you started using an icon set because it looked cool, then you realized it didn't have an icon for "upload" or "download".

The UI review meeting is later on today and you'd better get an icon in there quick! So, you use ▲ and ▼ instead. Except, they look totally different to the rest of the app and users have to spend those extra few seconds working out that, yes, they are actually part of the UI too.

Don't be lazy when it comes to icons: pick a metaphor and stick with it. This may mean extra illustration effort to produce new icon elements that are in keeping with the icon style, but that effort will pay off in increased usability for the end user.

Learning points

- Use a consistent icon style across the product
- Don't take a shortcut by including disparate icons
- Take the extra time to build a coherent icon style

#29

DON'T USE
OBSOLETE ICONS

For about 20 years, the "floppy diskette" icon has meant "save" and this connection still persists in UI across desktop and web apps. It was a great visual metaphor for a long time, but things have changed and many users under the age of 20 will have never laid eyes on a floppy disk.

Other examples include old telephones with handsets, curly cords and rotary dials; radio microphones from the 1950s; and reel-to-reel tape recorder icons to mean "voicemail".

Ten years from now, nobody will know what any of these are

Try to think about how the visual metaphors you use will work for different age groups, cultures and languages. Searching for the right visual metaphor for an icon is hard but rewarding, and your users will benefit from increased familiarity with your product. As designers, we're in need of a new standardized icon for "saving" (which these days means sending your data to a web-based service), rather than a removable or hard disk.

"Save to the cloud," perhaps? Icon by The Noun Project/Jeevan Kumar

Icons will always have a degree of ambiguity, but they should always be shown with a text label to reduce this (see *#32, Always Give Icons a Text Label*). The icon should serve primarily as a visual cue or shorthand, as well as a tappable (or clickable) target.

Like most things in design, icon selection benefits from testing with real users (refer to *#101, Test with Real Users*). Ask users what they think a proposed icon means to them and see if they can recall your icon later.

Learning points

- Don't use icons that depict obsolete technologies or visual metaphors
- Always show icons with a text label to reduce ambiguity
- Test your icons with real users

#30

**DON'T TRY TO DEPICT
A NEW IDEA WITH
AN EXISTING ICON**

Occasionally, you'll need to invent a whole new icon. If the concept you're trying to describe is novel, then your users will need an icon that doesn't confuse them by referencing another idea. It needs to be new, yet recognizable, and mappable onto a real-world example. If this sounds difficult to you, that's because it is.

Thankfully, the need to create an entirely new icon is very rare because most of the concepts in your app will be better served by existing UX patterns and UI conventions, but there may be a case where you have a new concept.

The middle ground here (using an existing icon to depict a new concept) is the worst of all worlds: it's confusing for users who have seen the icon before in other products, with a different meaning behind it.

Spare a thought for these poor guys...

Some of the most misused icons in this category are:

- The WiFi "fan" icon
- The generic "cloud" icon
- The globe icon

These icons can be seen frequently depicting ideas as diverse as "upload", "save", "share", "email", and so on. I've seen the WiFi icon being used to depict "pay with your contactless card." It's jarring and utterly confusing.

It's understandable that sometimes mistakes are made, but too often this is simply laziness: it can be hard to find the right icon and even harder to create a new one.

There are many large searchable directories of icons online (some of them are royalty-free, like my favorite at the moment, called `The Noun Project`, (https://thenounproject.com/)) and it's always worth a quick search on such sites to see what other designers have used to depict concepts.

This is another case where copying the patterns of others (many of these icons are available for reuse without a fee) is great for the user: they will be familiar with the patterns from other applications and uses, and you can save them learning and cognitive time by reusing these icons.

Learning points

- There's probably an icon out there that suits your needs already
- Don't use an existing icon for a new concept
- Check whether there are open source or public domain icons already

#31

**NEVER USE
TEXT ON ICONS**

Icons are *supposed* to be simple pictures that depict a concept. They are a shorthand visual reminder for users that what they're about to click is the thing they want.

Often, icon designers get frustrated that their pictogram isn't *quite right*, as it isn't quite recognizable or distinct enough. Instead of solving the problems with the picture, they opt to simply add a line of text *into the icon design*. Note that I'm not talking about text labels for icons—those are essential—I'm referring to the shady practice of including text *within* the icon itself.

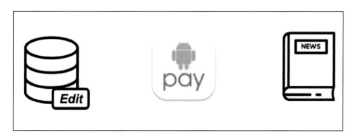

Three icons with text as part of the icon

First off, this is lazy design, but secondly, and more importantly, it breaks translation and accessibility functionality. Whether your product is a website, which can be translated with an online service like Google Translate, or a self-contained app, which will be internationalized with "strings" of copy, the text in icons won't get translated and users will get confused.

Users with accessibility needs who are using screen-reading software, will run into problems too: the software won't be able to "speak" text that's included on the icon. Spend that extra bit of time and effort building (or sourcing) icons that convey their meaning without text.

Learning points

- Don't include text inside icons
- Text within an icon can't be translated or read with assistive technologies
- Include text *labels* with icons but not text *in the icon itself*

#32

ALWAYS GIVE ICONS A TEXT LABEL

Now, I *don't* mean text on the icon (see *#29, Don't Use Obsolete Icons*)—I mean a text label *near* the icon, not just an icon on a button on its own. Small, nondescript buttons, with obscure mystery icons on them, are next to useless and consistently perform terribly in user tests. There are exceptions to this— frequently-used controls (like bold, italic, underline, and so on.) can be recognized without a text label, but icons in a main menu or toolbar really need descriptive text next to them.

Let's go back to the original purpose of the icon—to provide a quick visual shorthand by which the user can instantly recognize a control, and to provide a target for the user to click or tap. The icon isn't meant to describe a button the first time that the user sees it—the user will need a text label for that. However, if the icon is distinct and recognizable, then the user will locate the control and recall its purpose more quickly with an icon.

Which is easier to understand?

Icons are used and misused so relentlessly, across so many products, that you can't rely on any one single icon to convey a definitive meaning. For example, if you're offering a "history" feature—there's a wide range of pictogram clocks, arrows, clocks within arrows, hourglasses, and parchment scrolls to choose from—the user needs a text label to understand what *this* icon means in *this* context within your product.

Often, a designer will decide to sacrifice the icon label on mobile responsive views. Don't do this. Mobile users still need the label for context. The icon and the label will then work in tandem to provide context and instruction, and offer recall to the user, whether they're new to your product or use it every day.

Learning points

- Show text labels with icons at all times
- Don't hide or obscure labels on mobile versions
- Icons on their own are a major source of frustration for users

#33

**EMOJI ARE THE MOST
RECOGNIZED ICON
SET ON EARTH**

If your goal is to deliver interfaces with simple, usable icons that feel immediately familiar and intuitive, then use emoji.

Emoji have been used in Japan since the 1990s but Apple's iOS brought them to the Western world almost by accident —it had to support emoji for a deal with Japanese carrier SoftBank. Over time, Western users activated the international keyboard and began to use emoji. This culminated in Oxford Dictionaries naming "😂" as "word of the year" in 2015.

Put simply, the vast majority of people who use computer systems, smartphones, and tablets will be familiar with emoji.

They have a (relatively) standardized look across multiple platforms and there's a large range to choose from.

- 💡 **Idea**

  Get an idea from problems in your own life. If you don't have problems that are original enough, become a more original person. Don't build products that are solutions in search of a problem.

- 🛠 **Build**

  Build your idea with the tools you already know. Don't spend a year learning some language you'll never use. Don't outsource building to other people, that's a competitive disadvantage. Build only the core functionality. The rest comes later.

- 🚀 **Launch**

  Launch early and multiple times. Launch to famous startups websites (like Product Hunt, Hacker News, The Next Web), mainstream websites (like Reddit) and mainstream press (like Forbes). But also remember to find where your specific audience hangs out on the internet and launch there. Launch in a friendly way, that means "here's something I made that might be useful for you", instead of acting like you're some big giant new startup coming to change the world.

- 📈 **Grow**

  Grow organically. A great product that people really need which is better than the rest will pull people in. You don't need ads for that. Don't hire people if there's no revenue yet. Don't hire many people if there's revenue either. Stay lean and fast. Do things yourself.

- 💰 **Monetize**

  Monetize by asking users for money. Don't sell their data. Don't put ads

The *"MAKE"* book by Pieter Levels uses emoji well on its landing page

Simple, commonly used controls like media playback, have a complete icon set that the whole world understands, supported out of the box on every major platform:

Consider using emoji as part of your product's visual language.

Learning points

- Emoji might not be right for every situation, but they are extremely well-recognized and understood
- The vast majority of users of electronic devices will have encountered emoji at some point
- They can be used for extremely simple interactions, making them available to users who may be illiterate or have low reading ability

#34

USE DEVICE-NATIVE
INPUT FEATURES
WHERE POSSIBLE

If you're using a smartphone or tablet to dial a telephone number, the device's built-in "Phone" app will have a large numeric keypad that won't force you to use a fiddly QWERTY keyboard for numeric entry.

Sadly, too often, we ask users to use the wrong input features in our products. By leveraging what's already there, we can turn painful form entry experiences into effortless interactions.

The iOS "picker" control replaces fiddly drop-down menus

Drop-downs should let users use the device's full-width picker control and numeric entry should show a numeric keypad. For example, you can achieve the numeric keypad in web forms by adding the type=tel attribute to the input field in HTML. This will show the telephone keypad in both iOS and Android browsers:

The telephone keypad in Android

No matter how good you are, you can't justify spending the time and money that these companies have spent on making usable system controls. Even *if* you get it right, it's still yet another UI for your user to learn, when there's a perfectly good one already built into their device. Use that one.

Learning points

- Shortcut your way to success by using UI already built for you

- Using device-native input controls means that users have one less thing to learn

- This isn't just for mobile users: desktop software should use the right controls for those input methods

#35

OBFUSCATE PASSWORDS IN FIELDS, BUT PROVIDE A "SHOW PASSWORD" TOGGLE

It still makes sense to obfuscate ("star out") passwords as they're being entered, but let's be real, shoulder-surfing isn't possible when you're signing in to an app on your couch.

Providing a "show password" toggle is not only great for usability, but also improves security: users can enter longer, more complex pass-phrases and be confident that they can retype them correctly. Default to obfuscating the password, but provide a checkbox or toggle that allows the user to see their password.

Yes, I know we should all be using a password manager (a plugin that generates and stores all your site passwords for you), but the fact remains that most regular users don't.

Show the password strength rules. Don't make users try and try again to enter passwords, only to be told later that they need to have a certain obscure combination of letters, numbers and symbols. Show the user the rules the whole time that the password field is visible.

Finally, there's no need to force users to enter a password twice, just to check that they got the password correct. It slows users down, creates an unnecessary "test" for them to pass, and serves little purpose: if they did misspell their password, they can simply do a password reset later down the line.

Learning points

- Obfuscate passwords but let the user toggle them to visible

- Show the user any rules that they need to follow when creating a password

- Don't ask the user to retype the password when setting it

#36

ALWAYS ALLOW THE
USER TO PASTE INTO
PASSWORD FIELDS

It's difficult to fathom where this pattern of disabling paste came from or what possible security issue it's supposed to address. Using some JavaScript on the page to *prevent* users from pasting into a password field is *insane* and potentially harmful for security.

A user with a password manager app will have a long, impossible-to-remember password that has to be pasted into the field (especially on mobile, where it's more tricky to autofill the field).

It's a good general rule across the board to not interfere with standard system behaviors (copy, paste, find, zoom, right-click, and so on), as they are all basic interactions that the user will have grown accustomed to over years of working with various devices. To deliberately disable these behaviors on your product is nonsensical, yet it still happens. Designers think that they can improve security, reduce plagiarism, or other factors that aren't user-centric.

Back in the 1990s, "webmasters" would disable right-click to prevent users from copying images. This worked for about five seconds, until people realized that they could just screen capture the image.

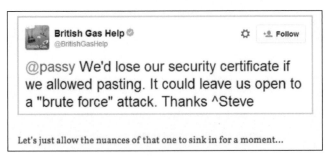

British Gas Help ✓
@BritishGasHelp   ☼   •♣ Follow

@passy We'd lose our security certificate if we allowed pasting. It could leave us open to a "brute force" attack. Thanks ^Steve

Let's just allow the nuances of that one to sink in for a moment...

Security expert Troy Hunt has lots to say (Troy Hunt (https://www.troyhunt.com/the-cobra-effect-that-is-disabling/): "The 'Cobra Effect' that is disabling paste on password fields.") on this phenomenon.

Disabling paste in a password field forces users to only use weak, easy-to-remember passwords. If you've disabled paste on a password field, then you need to have your laptop taken away from you.

Learning points

- Don't disable paste on password fields
- Don't interfere with any basic system interactions like copy, paste, find, and right-click
- Allow users to use password managers with your product

#37

DON'T ATTEMPT
TO VALIDATE
EMAIL ADDRESSES

Your user is entering an email address and you're thinking about writing some code to validate it (check that it's in a sensible format and they haven't entered gibberish or mistyped it). Think again.

It used to be so simple to validate email addresses on the client side. A little bit of JavaScript was all it took to check that the domain was in the format:

```
user@domain.tld
```

If it didn't match this pattern, it wasn't a valid email and the user couldn't sign up. We used to only have a handful of top-level domains (TLDs). Now, we have over 1,000 TLDs, with more being added all the time:

```
stealthy+user@example.ninja
```

```
holidays@🏠.ws
```

```
email@www.co
```

```
website@email.website
```

The above addresses are all valid domains*, but the TLD list changes all the time, so good luck writing the JavaScript to validate them—there are too many edge cases.

The side effect of this is that any errors will prevent legitimate users from signing up or using your product, leading to device-smashing levels of frustration and lost signups for your product.

Simply make your input field an "email" input (in HTML: `<input type="email">`) and let the browser and device figure the rest out (some will autofill or suggest the user's email address). You still may want to verify these addresses on the server side by sending a one-click link in an email to verify.

* Please don't email these people, in case they are real!

Learning points

- Don't validate emails on the client side
- Tell the browser or device that you're collecting an email address
- Verify emails on the server side with a one-click verification link

#38

DON'T EVER CLEAR
USER-ENTERED DATA
UNLESS SPECIFICALLY
ASKED TO

Your long-suffering user has painstakingly entered field after field of data into your form, often on a tiny mobile screen with an on screen keyboard. Don't clear this data unless the user specifically abandons the flow (maybe by hitting cancel). If clicking something is going to reload the page, and this might potentially fail, then make sure you save the user-entered data first.

This is an interesting example of where technical reality meets UX. On the one hand, if a browser could speak, it would likely argue that reloading a form *should* clear it, as we're literally telling the browser to fetch the empty form again. However, we're not robots, we're humans, and so much of good user experience design is about empathy and respect. This includes respecting the user's time and effort, and demonstrating empathy for what they're trying to achieve. Reloading a form with all the user's data removed is one of the lamest things you can do and nothing makes people angrier.

Learning points

- Don't ever clear user-entered data without explicit permission
- Treat the user's time with respect
- Put yourself in their shoes: would you want to type all this stuff in again?

#39

PICK A SENSIBLE SIZE FOR MULTILINE INPUT FIELDS

Forms need to be as frictionless as possible, because they are a huge barrier and conversion is low, so make them as easy for the user to complete as possible.

Sometimes, we need to ask users for more than a simple one- or two-word answer (like a name) and a multiline input field (or "text area") is needed. A common mistake on the web (and in some desktop apps) is to provide a text area that is way too big or way too small.

If the text area is way too big, and the user has to manipulate the viewport to see what they're typing, then you're wasting valuable screen space.

A text area that is way too big for the intended input

If the text area is way too small, then the user has to scroll around inside the field to see what they've written.

An impossibly small input field for lots of text

Think through the common responses in these fields and judge the size accordingly. This is a classic example of how a little UX thought before the UI design phase can massively improve the experience for most users.

Learning points

- Pick a sensible size based on how much text the user has to enter
- Don't just use default sizes: adjust them for each use case
- Consider these things early in the design phase

#40

DON'T EVER MAKE
YOUR UI MOVE
WHILE A USER
IS TRYING TO USE IT

Only a psychopath would deliberately make their UI move, forcing users to "press and guess" as they try to tap or click controls.

The prevalence of Flash on the web in the late 1990s and early 2000s led to many designers introducing UI animation just because they could, and it's almost always a bad idea. Unfortunately, UI can and does move due to unintentional factors and users are left frustrated.

Do these scenarios feel familiar? Have you had a web page load, but the advertising elements are served from a different, slower server? As the page loads, the introduction of these ads "shunts" the page elements around, meaning that you click or tap on the wrong part of the page.

This can be solved by testing, then introducing *placeholders* to reserve space for slow-loading elements, preventing the page from moving as it loads.

Maybe you're operating a control in a mobile app, when a time-sensitive notification appears— just under your finger as you go to tap something else—taking you out of your app and into another, unintended app. So-called "micro animations", where UI controls fade in and out as they're presented, or menus animate in or out, aren't necessarily a bad thing, as long as they're:

- Subtle, so as not to distract the user
- Short, so as not to interrupt the key task

UI control elements shouldn't move while the user is trying to use them.

I probably encounter these faults on a weekly basis, so, please, if you're asking users to control your software, don't make the controls move.

Learning points

- Keep UI control elements static
- Micro animations are fine, but keep them short and subtle
- Test how your interfaces appear on a range of devices and connection speeds

#41

USE THE SAME DATE PICKER CONTROLS CONSISTENTLY

This problem is less pronounced than it used to be, thanks to browsers and mobile device makers producing more consistent date picker UI. By triggering the device-native date picker, you can give the user an experience they're familiar with and a UI that has been designed for their device.

It's not always possible, however, as some tools need a more complex or more advanced interface for selecting dates, ranges of dates or comparison date ranges. When this is the case, always use the same date picker control everywhere in your app. Showing a *different* set of controls for the *same* task in a *different* part of your product will confuse users and reduce your conversion rates.

A common place that this mistake is made is on holiday or hotel booking sites. The home page will often have a big, clear date picker, designed to convert casual visitors into "searchers" when they land on the site. Once the user is deep into their journey, and they're asked to refine a date range, or pick flights or a hire car, that's when the bad UI creeps in and they're shown a *different* date picker.

Please be consistent with your UI—don't force your customer to learn yet another date picker. It might only take your user an extra second but respect your user's time. Life really is too short to wrestle with bad UI.

Learning points

- Use the same style of date picker across your product
- Using system-native controls can help to enforce this consistency
- Forcing users to adapt to multiple versions of the same control will confuse them and reduce your conversion rates

#42

PRE-FILL THE USERNAME IN "FORGOT PASSWORD" FIELDS

If your user has tried to log in and failed, it's a safe bet that their next action will be to click "forgot password." Don't make them enter their email again—pre-fill the username field with the entry from their earlier login, so the user can just tap "reset password" and be on their way.

The forgot password flow of an app is—certainly from metrics I've seen—a very well-used feature. In fact, a user who uses a difficult password, forgets it, then resets it every time, is probably more secure than a user who just uses a weak password. So, let's make the forgot password field easy by following these rules:

- If the user gets their password wrong, pre-fill the username field with the last-used username (or email) and show a "forgot password" button

- When they hit the button, email (or SMS) them a link that expires within a sensible time period

- The link, when tapped, should open a page for them to type a new password

- If the link is used more than once, it should still work (users accidentally double-click links often)

- When the new password is set, the user should be automatically signed in to the product

Reducing the frustration of not being able to sign in for returning users is a great move that will dramatically improve their experience.

Learning points

- A user doing a password reset has already given you their username, so reuse it
- Allow them to reset their password with a simple tap or click of a link
- Sign them in once the password is reset

#43

BE CASE-INSENSITIVE

Lots of systems are case-insensitive by default, but you don't notice it because that's how it should be and it works really well. For example, emailing `Will@WillGrant.org` goes to the same place as `will@willgrant.org`. Visiting `www.WikiPedia.ORG` takes you to the same site as `www.wikipedia.org`.

The email system and domain name system are both case-insensitive, which was a good call. Thousands of person-years of technical support time have likely been avoided by this decision.

Despite this, you can still find apps and websites where you have to sign in with a case-sensitive username or email address. Not only does this lead to errors—a user who can't sign in because their username had a capital letter they forgot about—but even if they *do* remember, switching between lowercase and uppercase letters on a fiddly mobile keyboard is a pain in the ass.

Misusing case-sensitivity creates a very *opaque* error for the user—they're usually not sure *why* it doesn't work and that's often the most frustrating type of error.

Passwords should always be case-sensitive. For everything else, default to case-insensitive unless you have a very good reason for case-sensitivity.

Learning points

- Default to case-insensitive if you're not sure
- Always make passwords case-sensitive
- If something has to be case-sensitive, tell the user this is the case

#44

**IF A GOOD FORM
EXPERIENCE CAN
BE DELIVERED,
YOUR USERS WILL
LOVE YOUR PRODUCT**

Almost every kind of software product features a form (a page with inputs for text, numbers and other data the user has to fill in). They are often the source of major frustration, but if you make your forms and data entry work well, your customers will thank you and your conversion rates will improve.

People generally hate filling in forms—it's slow and can be clunky and cumbersome—so let's make users' lives easier by streamlining and optimizing the data entry process.

This support request form asks for information that the system already knows

The first rule of Form Club is: don't ask for more information than you need. Time and again, users are asked to sign up to sites that ask for:

- First name
- Last name
- Middle initial
- Email address
- Title
- Organization
- Street address
- Town
- County
- State
- Postal code (ZIP code)
- Telephone number (home)
- Telephone number (cell)
- Telephone number (office)
- Password (with some arbitrary password complexity rules)
- Password (type it again)

At this point, your users are close to giving up joining your product or service. You just don't need all of this stuff. Your engineers might have designed the user tables to support it, and maybe your marketing people want it for demographics or direct mailing, but your users don't want it. Kill it.

In the ideal situation, a user should be able to join your product with:

- Email or cell phone number
- Password (only once—if they get it wrong, they can do a reset)

If you really need other stuff, then:

- Name (any number of names, separated by spaces). The user could add this to an optional profile, rather than it being part of mandatory onboarding.
- Address (house number, street and postal code/ ZIP code should be enough) but seriously, if you're not shipping physical items to the customer, why ask for this? It's organization-centric, not user-centric.

Asking your user to enter reams of information on forms is a surefire way to reduce conversion to a fraction-of-a-percentage level. If it's the kind of form they *have* to fill in, at least tell them why you're asking for the data and how it will be used. So many products get this wrong, so it's a great opportunity to deliver a good form experience and build a product that people love to use.

Read on for several form-related principles that may just change your life.

Learning points

- Don't ask for more information than you need
- Explain to the user why you're collecting it and what you will do with it
- Every additional field you add to a form reduces conversion

#45

VALIDATE DATA ENTRY AS SOON AS POSSIBLE

Validation on a form means showing the user visual feedback that there's a problem with some of the information they've painstakingly entered. Validate data entered into a field as soon as possible, when the user moves to the next field, so you know they're done typing in the current one.

Client-side validation isn't always technically possible, but you should aim for it wherever you can because the "round trip" to the server and back is frustrating if there are errors.

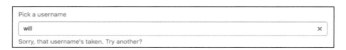

Tell the user to try again before they submit the form

There are lots of techniques for doing this, including plenty of third-party validation libraries for popular programming languages and frameworks. In the bad old days, the user would get a (sometimes partially-filled) form back after submitting, with errors marked in red like school homework.

Nowadays, it should be possible to show the user what they've done wrong (for example, too few digits for a phone number) and the steps they can take to rectify it.

The same goes for less common inputs like date pickers—they should include the logic to know that, for example, a hotel guest can't check out *before* they've been checked in. This is a simple bit of logic that can help you to avoid a whole raft of common problems.

Don't *ever* clear the form data just because the user made a mistake (see *#38, Don't Ever Clear User-Entered Data Unless Specifically Asked To*). There are bonus points for correcting common errors, for example, the user typing an email address ending `gmail.con` could see a suggestion: **"Did you mean gmail.com? Fix it for me!"**

Learning points

- Show the user where they've made mistakes as soon as possible
- Don't wait until the user has submitted the form
- You can't always validate without submitting the form, but it's a good principle to aim for

#46

IF THE FORM FAILS
VALIDATION, SHOW
THE USER WHICH
FIELD NEEDS THEIR
ATTENTION

If you really have to validate on the server side and can't do it on the client side (see *#45, Validate Data Entry as Soon as Possible*), then never send a user back to a form without telling them what to do next, and never with a generic message such as "there was an error."

The user will have likely entered several different bits of data and they'll need to get the context of the form back into their head again, once it comes back from server-side validation. The worst way to do this is by forcing them to scan the whole form again, looking for what they might have got wrong.

Highlight the problem (or problems) with the form and show the user where they need to correct items.

Showing the user exactly where their attention is needed

Sending the user back to an identical form to the one they just submitted, then expecting them to work out what went wrong—like some kind of puzzle—is the world's worst video game.

Learning points

- In server-side validation, there's a delay before the user gets feedback, so help them to remember the context

- Show the user exactly which areas need their attention

- Avoid generic "something is wrong" messages

#47

BE FORGIVING –
USERS DON'T KNOW
(AND DON'T CARE)
HOW YOU NEED
THE DATA

The overarching principle of both forms and wider UX could be summarized as "be forgiving."

Things that users do can often seem strange and unpredictable, but they probably have really good reasons:

- The user who can't save their name because it has a special character (like an accent or apostrophe)

- The user who can't enter a phone number because you're validating for phone number rules of the wrong locale

- The user who does (or doesn't) put spaces between groups of digits in their payment card number

- The user who spells their name with an emoji (this *will* happen)

Just because your developer set telephone fields to be 12 digits and 12 digits only, don't inflict this kind of madness on your poor users.

Your software should be forgiving—it should allow names to be comprised of multiple names, with hyphens and apostrophes. It should let users choose to skip non-mandatory fields. It should allow phone numbers with and without prefixes, and with extensions if users wish to enter them. It should allow users to enter postal codes in all manner of strange ways, for example, don't force them to enter (or omit) the space.

It's likely that some of these steps will create technical complexity or more work for your developers. There's no apology for this. Your product is there to serve the user, not to make life convenient for your internal development team.

Learning points

- Give your user flexibility in how they enter data
- Don't make your technical challenges a problem for the user
- Expect the user to do unpredictable things with your product

#48

PICK THE RIGHT CONTROL FOR THE JOB

UI designers have an extensive palette of controls and UI elements to choose from, so it's surprising to see, fairly often, poor choices of controls on forms.

You can enhance the UX of a product considerably by using the right control for the job. HTML5 has extensive form controls, supported by all modern browsers, including color pickers, telephone input, URL input with validation, and so on.

It's not always the most obvious control that you're looking for. Here are some examples:

- Showing users two radio buttons for a yes or no choice, when a checkbox or toggle switch would be simpler

- Overusing drop-down controls when there are only a few options (it would be better to use virtually any other control because a drop-down *obscures* the available choices from the user) see *#14, Don't Use a Drop-Down Menu If You Only Have a Few Options*

- "Build your own" UI for color selection when the HTML color input type is widely supported and shows a bespoke control suited to the user's device

Once again, this is an area where a little initial thought can save your users a lot of frustration.

Learning Points

- Consider whether you're using the best UI control for the job

- The most commonly-used approach may not be the best

- Don't build your own when there are standardized controls available to use

#49

ALLOW USERS
TO ENTER PHONE
NUMBERS HOWEVER
THEY WISH

Phone number entry should be as painless as possible for the user. Don't attempt to validate them, split them into groups of numbers, apply brackets or any of the other weird tricks you see all over the web. If you've tried to use a UK mobile number on a form that's demanding a European number, then you'll know the feeling.

My theory is that this sort of design comes from traditional paper form filling. Designers are tasked with copying or recreating what was once a paper form into the company's shiny new web application, but they take this too literally and users end up with a horrible experience as a result.

Stop and think whether a phone number is even necessary for most registration forms. I hate using the phone. The "Phone" app is my least favorite app on my phone (I've tried deleting it but it won't let me). However, I concede that there will be cases where you absolutely *have* to collect a phone number.

Carry out your clever phone number detection and parsing on the server side and let the user just simply key in their phone number. You get bonus marks for using `<input type="tel">`, which, on a mobile device, shows the telephone keypad when the field is tapped—and will show "Autofill" on modern smartphones—meaning that the user can add their number with one tap.

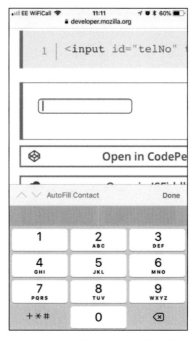

The numeric keypad being shown for a "tel" field

Learning points

- Don't attempt to validate or parse phone numbers in the user interface
- Just let the user key in their number
- Show the user a numeric keypad on mobile

#50

USE DROP
DOWNS SENSIBLY
FOR DATE ENTRY

A user entering a full date (like a date of birth) should be offered a drop down for the day and month, then a numeric entry for the year. Day and month are sufficiently short that a drop down doesn't feel too cumbersome. It also solves the issue of US dates having their day and month in the opposite order to most of Europe.

Don't use a drop down for the year though: it looks crazy and forcing the elderly to scroll back to the early 1900s seems very unfair. For mobile, use responsive design to show mobile users the date picker, a custom-designed UI on iOS and Android that makes picking dates a piece of cake.

Let's be real, would you rather build your own mobile date entry UI or stand on the shoulders of the designers at Apple and Google, who've done all the hard work for you?

The system-native date picker will also be familiar to users, reducing cognitive load and giving them one less thing to learn.

The iOS date picker

The date picker on Android

Learning points

- Use drop-down selectors for the day and month
- Use numeric entry for the year
- Mobile devices should show the system date picker

#51

CAPTURE THE BARE MINIMUM WHEN REQUESTING PAYMENT CARD DETAILS

The end goal for a lot of sites and apps is getting a user to pay. It's a cause for celebration: we've made something or are offering something so good that the user is happy to spend their hard-earned currency with us. So, why do we make it so hard for them to do so?

A credit or debit card number is already an unwieldy amount of data for a user to enter, so make it as easy as possible for them:

- Only collect what you need: card number, expiry and CV2 code.

- Allow the user to type the full card number into one field, but visually split it into groups of four digits as they enter it. This makes errors easier to spot but prevents the user having to move between four separate input fields.

- If the user hits the spacebar, then remove the space silently.

- Include some help text describing where to find the CV2 or card security code. It's not worth losing a customer because some people have different terms for this code.

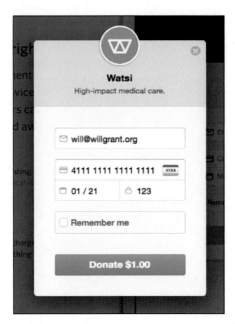

Stripe's default checkout behavior is pretty much perfect

If you don't need to collect the "valid from" date, issue number or postal/ZIP code—or 10 other random things—don't collect them. Every form field is another thing for the user to do, another bit of information to find and parse, and another chance for them to get stuck, change their mind, get bored or otherwise abandon your payment form.

Only ever collect card details over a HTTPS (secure) connection. Increasingly, browsers will alert the user if they're entering information into a non-secure page. There are services, such as `Let's Encrypt` (https://letsencrypt.org) (a free, automated, and open certificate authority), which allow you to generate a certificate free of charge.

Learning points

- Only collect the bare minimum of information you need to make the transaction
- Be forgiving: absorb accidental spaces and make numbers readable
- Only ever collect card details over a secure connection

#52

MAKE IT EASY FOR USERS TO ENTER POSTAL OR ZIP CODES

Postcodes and ZIP codes vary wildly around the world. Don't try to guess the format for the user: simply give them a text entry input field and allow them to enter their code. You can carry out validation if you need to on the server side. If you force users to enter a ZIP code, regardless of where they are in the world, expect a lot of junk ZIP codes in your database.

Some of the better forms that I've seen in recent years include a "live lookup", where entering a postcode (or part of a postcode) will return a list of possible address options for the user to tap or click. Obviously, this reduces the keystrokes and clicks that the user needs to make to enter their address and it also reduces error rates by pre-filling fields with data that has already been sanitized.

If you're dealing with a web page (as opposed to a native app, for example), then using the "Autocomplete" attribute on an input element in HTML will prompt some browsers to offer "Autofill" on that field:

```
<input autocomplete="shipping postal-code">
```

This will work in Android and iOS browsers, offering the user the chance to populate their own postcode in one tap.

Pre-filling the postcode with one tap

Bonus tip: country codes are often found at the end of a form, so don't let users enter all their data, then clear it because choosing a country changes the form's fields.

Learning points

- Form entry is a pain for users, so just let them enter their postcode simply and validate it later
- Offer a "live lookup" for postcodes to address conversion, if possible
- Allow "Autocomplete" in form fields using HTML

#53

DON'T ADD
DECIMAL PLACES
TO CURRENCY INPUT

This is yet another example where keeping it simple is the best option. Many currency input situations (sending a bank payment or adding a tip, for example) require the user to enter a value, which could be a whole amount ($10) or an arbitrary amount (£5.99).

Products sometimes try to be too helpful by auto-adding the decimal place or adding ".00" to the end of the value, which tends to lead to errors. Not the fun kind of errors either, but the kind where you bid $1000.00 for some underpants on eBay when you meant to offer $10.00 for them, maximum.

Allow the user to type the decimal themselves, but assume a ".00" if they don't.

 Pro-tip: After the entry is done, always present the value *back* to the user, so they can hit "confirm" or go back and edit it.

Learning points

- Don't add decimal places to currency entry, as it can lead to errors

- Allow the user to type the cents if they wish, but assume "0" if they don't

- Always ask the user to confirm the amount after entry

#54

**MAKE IT PAINLESS
FOR THE USER TO
ADD IMAGES**

There are a lot of situations in web and mobile apps where the user is asked to upload an image. It's done in a variety of ways, but here are some principles for getting user input in the form of images:

- Give the user the choice of picking a file or taking a picture, which is especially useful on mobile or tablet, where the request can trigger the system image picker, which has more functionality than your app can provide.

- Consider whether you would like the user to upload multiple images. If so, allow them to do this in one go, rather than lots of separate selections.

- Give the user "crop" and "rotate" controls when the image is previewed. It's super useful to be able to trim and rotate an image with a couple of clicks, rather than using another tool to do so.

- Try to accept a wide variety of image formats: JPEG, PNG and GIF at the very least.

- Tell the user that the image is uploading and show them the progress (uploads can be slow).

- For avatar images, consider using a third-party service like Gravatar, which should mean a good proportion of your users won't need to add an image at all. After all, the best interface is no interface.

Learning points

- Use device features for capturing images if they're available
- Allow multiple image uploads in one go if you want to collect more than one image
- Keep the user informed about the upload progress

#55

USE A "LINEAR" PROGRESS BAR IF A TASK WILL TAKE A DETERMINATE AMOUNT OF TIME

Despite your iPhone having the number-crunching power of a late-1990s supercomputer, everyday tasks still seem to take a maddeningly long time in a lot of software. Printing, for example: why does it take *so long* for the computer to send a document to a printer? It's as if the printer has to work out how to be a printer every time. Regardless, it's a great idea to let users know how long they're going to be waiting for.

Never show a series of completing progress bars, for example:

- Copying: 0...10..50..100%

- Decompressing: 0..20...60..100%

- Installing: 0...15...45...80...100%

- Finishing up: 0...20...60...100%

That should have just been *one* progress bar:

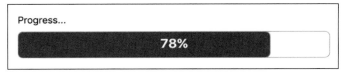

The perfect progress bar

A progress bar with a start and end, that gradually fills as the task completes, is the gold standard for this. There's no ambiguity and the user can get a good idea of how long this task will take, and that it's proceeding as planned.

In this case, by the word determinate, I mean that your software "knows" the number of things it has to do (or can work it out), and can work through them while updating on progress. Default to this option if you can.

Learning points

- Show a linear progress bar if your software is able to
- Show only one progress bar for the whole operation
- Give the progress bar a clear start and end

#56

SHOW A "SPINNER"
IF THE TASK WILL TAKE
AN INDETERMINATE
AMOUNT OF TIME

In this case, by indeterminate, I mean that your software isn't sure (or has no way of knowing) how many things it has to do: it just knows that it will know when it is done.

Showing an animated spinner gives a user less information than a progress bar, but it at least tells them that something is happening and their task will be done when the spinner vanishes.

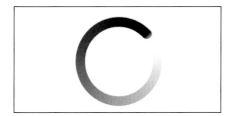

A spinner. Other styles are available

If something goes wrong, then make the spinner stop. Your user doesn't know whether this is a "loop forever" GIF, so they'll just carry on waiting when nothing is actually happening behind the scenes. Gmail shows "loading" and then, after some time, it shows "still loading", which is a nice touch.

A spinner is also great for tasks that are very short, for example a page reload, where a progress bar would be overkill.

Learning points

- Use a spinner when your product can't reliably show a progress bar
- Use animation to indicate that something is happening
- Stop or remove the spinner if something goes wrong

#57

NEVER SHOW AN ANIMATED, LOOPING PROGRESS BAR

Some of the most awful (and hilarious) UI disasters that I've come across have this particular travesty in common. An animated (often a GIF) progress bar which, once it has meandered its way to the end, restarts back at zero and does it all over again is common. Think of it as a "linear spinner". If you really dislike your users, then this is an excellent way to "troll" them.

Animated progress bars could actually be a symptom of developers testing things locally on their computers, rather than on the wider internet. Everything loads so quickly during local testing that a developer may never see a progress bar. This is yet another vote for testing in the real world with real users (refer to *#101, Test with Real Users*).

Learning points

- Don't show a looping progress bar
- Don't indicate to users that something is about to complete when it isn't
- Test your software in real internet conditions, not just on your computer

#58

SHOW A NUMERIC PROGRESS INDICATOR ON THE PROGRESS BAR

Show a numeric (percentage) indicator on the progress bar, but only if there's time to read it.

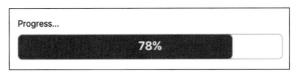

A progress bar with a numeric indicator

A progress bar and a number that appears for a fraction of a second is just confusing and adds to the visual clutter that the user needs to process. If they're going to be stuck looking at the progress bar for a few seconds, then a percentage is a nice, universally-understood way of keeping them updated.

Also, this numeric indicator could be an amount of time. So, for an update, you can show a certain amount of minutes remaining. However, a percentage is more useful for shorter processes. Be careful because calculating "time remaining" is often a big technical challenge. It's pretty common to see an update say "24 minutes remaining" and then see it complete in the next few seconds. If you're not confident that you're giving users an accurate time, then it's better to leave it out and use a percentage instead.

That's it, the captivating progress bar section is over. Now, if we can all *please* get progress bars right over the next few years, I might not need to write about them again!

Learning points

- Show a "percentage complete" numeric indicator on a progress bar, if there's time to read it

- For long processes, consider showing time remaining

- If you can't show an accurate estimate of time remaining, just revert to a percentage

#59

CONTRAST RATIOS
ARE YOUR FRIENDS

Way back in 1999, the World **Wide Web Consortium (W3C)**, the main international standards organization for the internet, published the catchily-titled "Web Content Accessibility Guidelines" (or **WCAG**). They were revised and updated to "WCAG 2.0" in 2008, with the guidelines stating that "websites must be perceivable, operable, understandable, and robust."

The guidelines are extensive and detailed, and go way beyond the scope of this book, but some key elements from them are great best-practice guidelines to incorporate into your UX work.

One great guideline is that on contrast:

1.4.3 Contrast (Minimum): The visual presentation of text and images of text has a contrast ratio of at least 4.5:1.

There are some exemptions and caveats around logos and especially large text, but the "golden rule" contrast ratio of 4.5:1 is one to live by. See the three example buttons below. The low-contrast button would be really hard to use for partially-sighted people.

What's more, people with perfect vision would also find it annoying and difficult to read (especially on a tiny mobile screen).

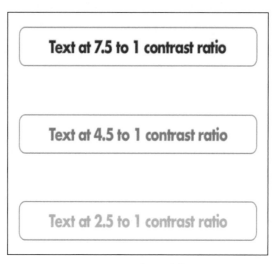

Text at 7.5 to 1 contrast ratio

Text at 4.5 to 1 contrast ratio

Text at 2.5 to 1 contrast ratio

How contrast makes a difference

There are automated contrast checkers on the web, so search for one in your favorite search engine and give it a whirl on your UI contrast. A decent contrast ratio will help partially-sighted people, as well as preventing fully-sighted users from getting frustrated.

Remember, if the marketing team tells you that text on controls or in-app copy *has* to be in a low-contrast color combination for branding reasons, then tell them where to shove their brand guide!

Learning points

- A contrast ratio of 4.1:1 is an absolute minimum
- Aim for a contrast ratio of around 7.5:1 for maximum readability
- Like many accessibility tweaks, this one benefits all users, regardless of their ability

#60

IF YOU MUST USE "FLAT DESIGN" THEN ADD SOME VISUAL AFFORDANCES TO CONTROLS

Minimalism is generally good and reducing clutter and visual distractions can often help a user to find what he or she needs more quickly. Minimalism does not, however, mean making controls so minimal that they are impossible to use.

The flat design aesthetic (refer to *#7, Make Your Buttons Look Like Buttons*) tends to remove visual affordances, but not to the same extent as the newly-emerging "web brutalism." Brutalism, inspired by the brutalist architectural style, is an aesthetic in product design that deliberately looks *unstyled* and raw (Craigslist is a great example).

Outside of being a *joke for designers*, this level of minimalism is too imposing and unnecessary and, like flat design, can degrade discoverability by removing all visual affordances.

Let's look at some UI in the widely-used Google Calendar (iOS) app. The strict adherence to flat design here means that it's very hard to work out what is *tappable* and what isn't.

The Google calendar app

It's good that less frequently used controls (like "email" and "delete") are hidden from most users, but they're not discoverable: the menu to find them is a small, unlabeled "ellipsis" menu in the top right.

There's also a problem with consistency. The "pencil" edit icon is tappable and has a subtle drop shadow (a visual affordance!), but none of the other tappable items do.

Compare Google Calendar to a section of the user interface from the following control panel of `Stripe.com` (http://Stripe.com).

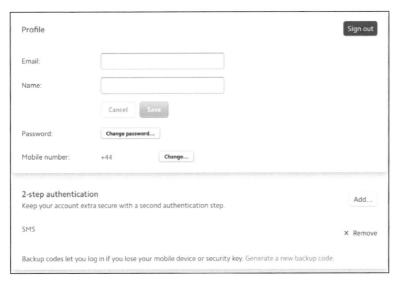

Stripe.com's control panel

It strikes a great balance between minimalism and affordances. It's clean and simple, and here are some of the reasons why:

- It's broken down into logical sections
- The controls are clearly recognizable as tappable
- An **"X icon"** is used for **Remove**, but it is labeled with some text
- The **Add...** button features an ellipsis, indicating that there's another step to be completed when it's clicked

It's not perfect (the button styles are a little inconsistent, for example), but overall it's a better interface than the Google Calendar. I guarantee that users will have a better experience with this UI than with Google's.

Learning points

- Visual affordances on controls are still vital for all user interfaces
- Consistency across your product will help users to learn your interface more quickly
- Don't take minimalism too far: find a balance

#61

AVOID AMBIGUOUS SYMBOLS

This is easier said than done, but there are some symbols and iconography that are often used and misused across products. Here are just a couple of examples from products on the web and mobile, but there are hundreds more:

- @: The "at" symbol is a repeat offender in the context of the control. Does it mean "email", a web link or something else?

- ↱: Does this mean "share" or "new window" or "open additional menu options"? I've seen it used to represent all of the above, as well as upside down to mean "go back".

Some things to think about when picking iconography:

- Is there a well-used existing icon for this which can be reused? Users will already know it and you don't have to redesign it.

- Is this proposed icon distinct from the others and memorable?

- Does this proposed icon conflict with any established patterns?

By giving your iconography and symbols a bit of extra thought, you can help to make your interface—and, therefore, your user's experience—a whole lot better.

Learning points

- Choose your icons with care and thought
- Don't reinvent the wheel: there's probably an established pattern that you can reuse
- Icons are like jokes: if you have to explain them, they've not worked

#62

**MAKE LINKS
MAKE SENSE
OUT OF CONTEXT**

Q: What's the difference between these two ways of offering a web link to a user?

- To download our brochure: `click here`.
- You can `download our brochure` here.

A: The first one is harder for visually impaired people to use.

Screen-reader software often has a mode where the user can "skim" the page for clickable links, and these links need to make sense out of context. In this case, the first link would be read aloud as "click here", while the second would be dictated as "download our brochure"—much more usable.

Let's take another example from an index of blog posts:

- Blog post story 1

  `Read more`

  or

- Blog post item 2

  `Read blog post item 2`

In this example, recapping the title in the "read more" link gives additional context and prevents the screen reader from simply reading a list of "read more, read more" over and over.

[**Bonus**: Making your links descriptive can help some search indexes to make sense of your content.]

Learning points

- Avoid "click here" links
- Use descriptive links that make sense out of context
- This will help with search indexing as well as accessibility

#63

ADD "SKIP TO CONTENT" LINKS ABOVE THE HEADER AND NAVIGATION

As previously mentioned, some users with a visual impairment will be using screen-reader technology to read the text elements of your interface aloud.

One problem is that it's easy for these users to get lost in the mess of links and content on an especially-busy page. Users need a way to get to the navigation. For fully-sighted users, the location of the navigation is a well-accepted pattern, but partially-sighted users may not have the same "mental model" of a web page or web app.

Adding a "skip to content" link to the top of your site (it need only be visible to screen readers) will allow the user to skip past the navigation effortlessly. They don't want to have to hear all your menu options read aloud, over and over, each time a page is loaded.

Here's the CSS that the W3C recommends using to position the link off-screen for sighted users:

```
#skiptocontent {
  height: 1px;
  width: 1px;
  position: absolute;
  overflow: hidden;
  top: -10px;
}
```

Learning points

- Add a "skip to content" link to the top of your site
- Use CSS positioning to hide the link for sighted users
- Include this in your site or app templates, so it appears on every page automatically

#64

DON'T ONLY USE COLOR TO CONVEY INFORMATION

This sounds counterintuitive: making a warning red or a success alert green is second nature to most designers. While color can act as a shorthand for most users, those with color blindness can find themselves at a disadvantage. Certain types of color blindness will mean that users can't tell the difference between a red status blob and a green one.

The best way to approach this is to use color to convey *additional* information, and not just use color alone. This makes the site usable for the vast majority of people, but not at the expense of a few. This is why I advise making links underlined (and, optionally, a different color), not *just* a different color, to differentiate them from body copy.

For example, a "status normal" label could show a green indicator blob, but should never *just* be the green blob on its own.

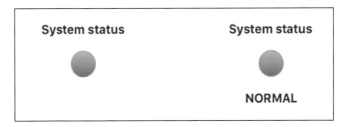

Only one of these interfaces is usable for color-blind people

Color is a great secondary indicator: a visual cue that will help people to identify elements of your product more quickly and get information simply. This principle is intended to remind you that not everyone can see colors (there are 27 million people with some form of color blindness in the US alone), so it shouldn't be the only way of conveying a message.

Learning points:

- Don't use color on its own to convey information
- Ensure that there are other indicators along with color
- Color is still a great secondary source of information for users

#65

IF YOU TURN
OFF DEVICE ZOOM
WITH A META TAG,
YOU'RE EVIL

```
<meta name="viewport" content="width=device-
width, initial-scale=1.0, maximum-scale=1.0, user-
scalable=no" />
```

Adding this meta tag to the head of an HTML page will prevent the user from scaling the page, either using their browser controls or with "pinch-to-zoom" on a touchscreen device. This also prevents users with vision difficulties from scaling the page.

Although rare, it's still seen in the wild. Designers typically do this because:

- They haven't made their designs work responsively or don't know how to
- They don't understand the implications for accessibility
- They are stupid

Don't be these designers. Let your users choose how to view and manipulate your interfaces. Away from web pages, offer these scaling controls in desktop and native mobile software. iOS and Android both have built-in support for accessibility features that you can hook into and, as a result, respect the user's preferences for type size and contrast.

A designer can't ever know how a user will want to view their content, so don't assume. Not being able to design a "pixel-perfect" outcome for every device size means that pulling these kinds of tricks (disabling scale, for example) is simply shooting yourself in the foot. As with most adjustments for accessibility, responsive content creates a better experience for all users, regardless of ability.

Learning points

- Let go of pixel-perfect design and accept that users will want to view your products on their terms
- Use device-native accessibility features where you can
- Test your product's interfaces on multiple device sizes and with assistive technologies

#66

GIVE NAVIGATION ELEMENTS A LOGICAL TAB ORDER

Try an experiment: head to a website in your browser and start pressing the *Tab* key. You should notice the "focus" (usually a colored rectangle or shaded area) move from item to item across the site.

This is one of the ways that users who are partially sighted, or have motion difficulties, use web pages. These users rely on interface designers to use common sense in the tab order that they assign to items. On some websites and web apps this is horrible, while on some it's clearly been well thought through.

Filling in a form is often extra frustrating when tapping the *Tab* key takes your focus to a strange part of the page. It's unlikely that you'll be writing code yourself, but you may wish to tell your frontend developers that they can specify the order that items are selected in using the tabindex attribute:

```
<input type="text" name="field1" tabindex=1 />
<input type="text" name="field2" tabindex=2 />
```

For navigation and menus, it's important that you check through them and ensure that they are in a logical order. Your customers using assistive technologies will thank you.

Learning points

- Ensure that tabbing around your UI takes the focus in a sensible direction
- Although this is especially important for accessibility, all users will benefit from forms that are easier to move around
- Test your designs with assistive technologies

#67

WRITE CLEAR LABELS FOR CONTROLS

Another small change you can make, which will make the world of difference to your users using assistive technologies, is writing clear labels:

Bad:

```
┌─────────────────────────────────────────────────────┐
│                                                       │
│   ┌─────────────────────────────────────────────┐    │
│   │ Firstname Lastname                          │    │
│   └─────────────────────────────────────────────┘    │
│                        ┌──────────┐  ┌──────────┐     │
│                        │  Cancel  │  │  Save   │      │
│                        └──────────┘  └──────────┘     │
│                                                       │
└─────────────────────────────────────────────────────┘
```

Good:

```
┌─────────────────────────────────────────────────────┐
│      Your full name                                   │
│   ┌─────────────────────────────────────────────┐    │
│   │                                             │    │
│   └─────────────────────────────────────────────┘    │
│                        ┌──────────┐  ┌──────────┐     │
│                        │  Cancel  │  │  Save   │      │
│                        └──────────┘  └──────────┘     │
│                                                       │
└─────────────────────────────────────────────────────┘
```

Pre-filling your field with "placeholder" (or "watermark") text may look tidy, but it's not supported in all browsers, and disappears when the focus moves to the input field.

You can, however, include **both**, which allows the field to be identified and gives some assistance to users as to the kind of information that is needed for that input.

An input with a clear label and a helpful watermark

I know I've tapped a field many times, planning to type some information in, only to stop and think, "Wait, what was this field for?" Yet again, this is an example of improving accessibility (screen readers use labels to make forms usable), while also improving the overall experience for your whole audience.

Learning points

- Screen readers rely on labels for partially-sighted users
- Field labels benefit all users
- Placeholder labels disappear or are obscured when the user types in the field

#68

LET USERS TURN
OFF SPECIFIC
NOTIFICATIONS

Notifications, whether on desktop or, more commonly, mobile, are a great way to keep users informed of state changes while the app is closed or in the background.

It's worth thinking through carefully how users can customize or disable certain types of notifications (or all of them). The events that each user considers important, or notification-worthy, will vary and may even change over time.

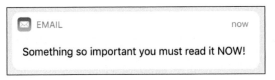

A notification

A user probably doesn't want an audio notification every time someone likes their Instagram selfie. Perhaps they *do* want a notification of a direct message because they get them less frequently.

The user's device or browser will allow them to disable notifications entirely for your app, which they will most likely do if what they're seeing isn't fine-tuned enough. It's extra technical work to allow a user this kind of fine-grained control, but allowing them to set up notifications how they want them is a serious advantage over your competitors' products.

There's an approach, particularly in mobile products, that seems to advocate bombarding users with as many push notifications as possible, to encourage repeat usage. In my experience, this does more harm than good to your product in terms of UX and retention.

An added bonus is that by allowing a user fine-grained control over these notifications, they are going to be happier with your app's "noise level" and will be less likely to disable notifications at a system level.

Learning points

- Allow users fine-grained control over notifications
- Don't bombard users with too many messages
- Remember that users can simply disable all notifications for your product at a system level

#69

MAKE TAPPABLE
AREAS FINGER-SIZED

If you think your design will be used by touch, then your users' fingers are the tool that they'll use. Given that obvious statement, it's surprising to see UI controls in touch interfaces that are clearly *way too small* for users to poke at easily with their digits.

As a guide, your smartphone screen is (roughly) five fingers wide and 10 fingers high, so that's about the limit of the controls that can be comfortably used on such a display. If you were to try to fit more than five items horizontally across the display, they would be too small to be comfortably used.

You'll need to experiment to find the right control size, but if you're using native control elements (see *#34, Use Device-Native Input Features Where Possible*), that research has been done for you: they're already the right size.

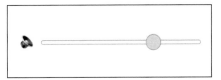

Make controls a size that humans can operate with their fingers

If you're building your own touchscreen controls, use the human finger size as a guide. Trying to grab a 1 or 2 pixel-sized control with a finger is needlessly difficult and will frustrate users no end.

Don't make elements adjacent if some users will be accessing your product via touch. Padding between buttons prevents the wrong button from being touched accidentally. 2mm is a good guide for padding, in however many pixels that means for your display.

Learning points

- Think about the size of human fingers when designing touch interfaces
- Don't make touch controls too small for users to use comfortably
- Add padding between control elements to prevent accidental mis-taps

#70

A USER'S JOURNEY
SHOULD HAVE
A BEGINNING,
MIDDLE, AND END

The user's journey can be thought of in a broad or narrow way: it can be their journey through the whole product—for a dating app that could be from signing up to a first date—or it could be a fine-grained journey, for example, into a particular settings menu to change an option.

As the user goes through their "jobs to be done", they make a great many small journeys. In every case, the user should know that they have begun a journey, that that journey will end at some point, and when it has ended.

The classic anti-pattern here is users thinking, "Have I saved these settings or not?" On macOS, changing the settings and then closing the window saves the settings, while on (older) Windows applications, the user must press "save". In some more obscure systems, the user must click **apply** and then **save**.

The user is never sure whether this journey (to change a setting) has ended or not, so make it clear to them.

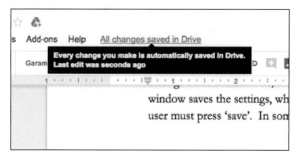

Making an edit to a Google doc lets you know that the change has been saved

MailChimp gives you a high five from a chimp so you're sure it's worked

Keeping users updated with the right amount of clear communication is not an easy task—and every product is different—but it's worth testing your journeys to ensure that these signposts are visible along the way.

Learning points

- It can help to think of user tasks and journeys as needing signposts along the way
- Keep the user informed as to when they've finished doing the task they're trying to do
- Some examples of end-of-journey signposts include "message sent", "changes saved", and "link posted"

#71

THE USER SHOULD ALWAYS KNOW AT WHAT STAGE THEY ARE IN ANY GIVEN JOURNEY

Some of the worst experiences in digital products come from not adhering to this principle. For example, an item that hasn't been ordered because the user didn't click **confirm**, or the user who simply can't find parts of the product because they're buried too deeply, with no affordances.

Most users will approach your product with an incomplete (or non-existent) conceptual model of how it functions. You need to expose some of this to the user, so they can understand how to use the product.

Although the user will not consciously "know" what stage they're at, at all times they should at least have a general sense of it and you can deliver that experience with some simple cues.

Much like landmarks in the real world, your product should include visually different areas that serve as landmarks in the product. The home screen should look different to the settings screen, for example. Although it sounds obvious, making screens look visually distinct will help the user to think, "I'm back at the home page." This contributes to an overall feeling of control for the user, reinforcing their mental model.

Some of the ways you can expose the user's stage in a journey include:

- A segmented progress indicator
- A "breadcrumb" control (see *#72, Use Breadcrumb Navigation*)
- An indicator that shows their work hasn't (or has) been saved
- With words—explain to the user what they've done and what comes next

Stop making users feel disorientated: give them some cues—visual or otherwise—to help them to feel their place in each journey.

Learning points

- Provide visual cues that serve as landmarks in the product
- Tell the user clearly what stage they're at in every journey
- Give the user controls that let them move between stages

#72

USE BREADCRUMB NAVIGATION

The breadcrumb is not the sexiest of UI components, but it's a long-standing, tried-and-tested control that your users will turn to again and again.

Home > Products > Apparel > Hoodies

Websites and apps on the desktop and tablet (and often mobile) can fit a small and unobtrusive breadcrumb into their UI with ease. They are *almost never* misunderstood by users in testing and real-world use.

The breadcrumb allows your user to see his or her position in the system and easily return to a previous level of the hierarchy. What's more, by displaying the path the user took to get to their current location, breadcrumb navigation helps the user to form a better mental model of the layout of the product.

Increasingly, in the world of single-page JavaScript apps, we're seeing breadcrumbs overlooked in the design phase, perhaps because they're seen as boring (they're one of the earliest inventions of web UI).

Overlooking breadcrumb navigation is a huge own goal for your product's usability. Breadcrumbs also remove the need for a back button in your product, which should always be avoided, as it replicates existing browser functionality in a non-standard, site-by-site way.

It's vital to remember that your job as a UX professional is not to follow trends and remove breadcrumbs just because the control is seen by some as "old school". Your job is to improve usability and this is a great way of doing it with very little screen space and at no detriment to users who overlook it.

Learning points

- Use breadcrumb navigation to help your user to both move around and understand your product
- Consider whether the breadcrumb is required on mobile—it might not always be needed
- Breadcrumbs are well understood by a wide audience of users

#73

IF THE USER IS ON AN
OPTIONAL JOURNEY,
GIVE THEM A CONTROL
TO "SKIP THIS"

Not all journeys are linear and not all steps along a journey are necessary. It's a very frustrating experience to be "trapped" in a digital product— forced to complete a journey or task you know you need to skip but with no way out.

This principle is simple—allow your user to "skip this" any time it's possible to do so. The archetypal example of this is during an "onboarding" wizard where, if it's not actually the first time you've used the product, being forced to "learn" things you already know is simply infuriating.

The team messaging app Slack handles this well:

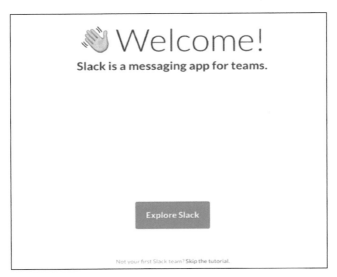

Slack asks if it's "Not your first Slack team?"

The **Not your first Slack team?** text at the bottom of the view could be bigger and clearer, but it's there and most users will find it easily enough without going through the tutorial for the umpteenth time.

I do wonder why the "skip" text is so small in this example, but it's likely that Slack has used analytics to work out the proportion of visitors who are first-time versus returning users. This is a great example of how you should use metrics from your product to inform the design decisions you make.

Learning points

- Allow users to skip optional parts of journeys
- Don't trap users in non-essential parts of your product
- Use metrics from analytics to inform your design decisions

#74

USERS DON'T CARE ABOUT YOUR COMPANY

There's a running joke in the HBO series *Silicon Valley* about how every tech company wants to make the world a better place. The show's main antagonist Gavin Belson goes so far as to say, "I don't want to live in a world where someone else makes the world a better place better than we do."

Too many products labor the point: telling their users about their mission or vision, which is about how they're trying to change the world. Please don't do this because users simply don't care. Products are useful for what they let users *do*. This pattern of too much information is a symptom of a lack of objectivity.

If a user has installed your dating app, for example, the chances are that they have some clear goals in mind: some basic "jobs to be done" that involve setting up a profile and meeting people. They don't want a multi-screen onboarding wizard that tells them how your company "brings people together", complete with some stock photos of couples on beaches, holding hands.

When Google launched, it attracted users with its simple UI and high-quality search results.

The UI looked like this:

Old-school Google

Google had no "brand" to speak of, a pretty ugly logo, and no real corporate vision or mission statement. Google *did* have a killer feature: better search result relevance than all the competitors, which made it the winner.

As a UX professional, you have to "play nice" with other teams across the business, but this is one example where championing simplicity over complexity can really improve the experience for users. Once again, objectivity is the most important skill for a UX professional. Put yourself in your users' shoes.

Learning points

- Don't overdo the corporate vision in your product
- Users care about what your product lets them do, not what it says it does
- Strive for objectivity in your work

#75

FOLLOW THE STANDARD E-COMMERCE PATTERN

If you're selling items online—physical goods or digital items—then, like it or not, you're in the world of e-Commerce. The word e-Commerce seems hopelessly outdated, but it's the best word we've got to mean "selling things online through a website or app."

Now, because e-Commerce generates revenue for businesses in a very direct way, it was one of the first areas of online experience to really get deep focus and attention from UX professionals. Even marginal gains could increase revenue by significant volumes, so it was worth putting in the effort of user testing and A/B trials.

The "e-Commerce pattern" we've arrived at from the past 20 years of the consumer web is both well-refined and well-understood by users. Getting a customer through a purchase funnel is difficult, which means that it has to be as frictionless as possible, so make everything as familiar as possible.

It goes a little something like this:

- **Products**: Products are listed in categories, with attributes like price, size, color, pattern, and so on. Users can search and sort these products by their attributes. Viewing a product shows controls to adjust the size, color, and so on—if these options are available—as well as a quantity selector and an **add to basket** button, which adds the quantity selected to the basket. Depending on the type of item, the user may be prompted to go straight to the checkout (if they're only expected to buy one thing).

- **The basket**: The basket or cart shows the user the items and the quantity they've selected. From there, they can modify quantities, remove items, clear the basket or proceed to checkout.

- **The checkout**: The user is shown the total and asked to enter personal details like delivery address and payment information. If they have an account, they can optionally sign in at this stage (to avoid entering details over and over), but you should allow "guest checkout" where possible.

That's all there is to it! This is the tried-and-tested pattern that's sold billions of items over the years. You'd be crazy to mess with it.

Learning points

- Every way that you can reduce friction in the purchasing funnel will increase conversions
- Users expect your store to work like every other store they've used
- Follow the pattern of products, a shopping basket, and a checkout

#76

SHOW AN INDICATOR IN THE TITLE BAR IF THE USER'S WORK IS UNSAVED

If possible, your app should be "autosaving" the user's work, but there are, of course, cases where this needs to be a user-initiated action (for example, in a creative application where saving could be destructive).

A great way of showing the user that their work is unsaved is by displaying a visual indicator in the title bar of the app. This could be a bullet or could even explicitly say "not saved", if space allows.

At a glance, the user can tell if they need to quickly hit *cmd* + *S* (or *Ctrl* + *S*) to save where they're at or if they're just experimenting, they will know that they haven't saved.

A big part of this is about respecting the time and effort that the user has put into using your product: entering data, preparing a profile, or bio, and so on. They deserve to be shown the state that their work is in and not have to guess or remember whether it's saved or not.

Learning points

- Show the user whether their work has been saved or not
- Consider whether autosaving a user's work is helpful or not for your product
- Show your user that you respect the time and effort they've put into using your product

#77

DON'T NAG YOUR USERS INTO RATING YOUR APP

Your users probably come to your product for a wide range of reasons. Perhaps it makes their life easier or passes some time while they are on the bus or allows them to do something cool that they could never have done before.

Your users **didn't** come to your product to see this:

Nobody cares

This is the "rate this app" nag window that appears at the worst possible time.

As app stores became the huge industry that they are today, app developers and software publishers quickly learned that ratings are an essential part of the mix of signals that make their app rank higher in search results. Discoverability has historically been a problem on app stores and publishers will do anything they can to "game" the rankings and appear more prominently.

Your poor user is stuck in the middle, being constantly asked to rate apps. Another level of annoyance is a dark pattern of giving users a "do you like this app?" prompt, which then *only shows* the rate dialog if the user said "yes.

If a user **really** cares about your product, they'll write a positive or negative review, so including a link somewhere is fine. This full-screen nag window is designed to serve only the needs of your app and your organization, not the user. Please don't use them.

Learning points

- Don't get in the way of your user using the app
- Don't nag them into reviewing or rating your app
- Think about your user's needs ahead of the organization's needs

#78

DON'T USE A VANITY SPLASH SCREEN

The splash screen—the full-screen graphic that appears when your user opens your iOS or Android app—is a great place for your company logo, brand messaging, or corporate vision statement, right?

No. Do not do this.

Users do not care about your corporate vision statement (and how you're making the world a better place)—they just want to open the app to do whatever it is the app does.

Instead, look at the first screen of your app and offer a splash screen that echoes this layout, but without content. Users will feel like the app is loading quicker if they see the expected interface and it then transitions into the "real" interface.

Load the UI quickly, and if that means some user interactions aren't ready yet, only show the user a spinner if they click them. For example, in a word processor, let them start typing as soon as the app opens and load in the pretty "add a chart" dialog later, if the user clicks it. If there is a need for a dedicated login screen before the user sees anything else, some of this branding can be done there.

Learning points

- Don't show the user company information on a splash screen
- Help the user get into your product as quickly as possible
- Put the user's needs first, not your corporation's needs

#79

MAKE YOUR
FAVICON
DISTINCTIVE

A favicon, app icon or "apple-touch-icon"—whatever you call it—is an icon you may well have forgotten to add to your web app. It serves a useful purpose beyond branding.

Users with lots of tabs open, lots of apps in their start menu, or lots of apps in a folder on their phone, will appreciate being able to find yours quickly.

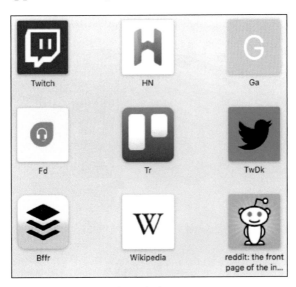

Some favicons

A bright, bold icon or letter is usually sufficient, but test it at 16 pixels in size to see that it's legible. Use transparency well, unless your icon actually is a square—nobody wants an ugly white square in their tab bar.

If users can see your app instantly and switch to it, you'll be saving thousands of hours of people's time cumulatively. Good job!

Learning points

- Make your favicon clear and distinctive
- Users use favicons to identify tabs, favorites, and more
- Favicons can be displayed as small as 16 pixels, so check them at that size

#80

ADD A "CREATE FROM EXISTING" FLOW

An often overlooked flow in many CRUD (stands for create, read, update, and delete. It refers to the standard set of actions that a user may want to perform on a set of database records. This can be users, customers, products, orders or just about anything else—(CRUD apps) (https://en.wikipedia.org/wiki/Create,_read,_update_and_delete)) apps is the "create from existing" flow. When given a list of items that they have meticulously created, this simple flow is a massive time saver and productivity boost for the user.

Selecting "create from existing," or "duplicate and edit," or even "duplicate," should make the product behave something like this:

- The user clicks "duplicate and edit"
- The system copies the item, giving it a new ID
- The user is presented with the edit view, but with a new name (perhaps with "copy" appended to the original title)
- The fields are pre-filled with the data from the original item
- The user can change as much or as little as they wish and click "save"

This flow is useful anywhere that a user is adding items or maintaining a list of items. It's fairly typical for business-to-business applications (for example, customer records, orders, and so on) to be comprised of a lot of detailed records. The flow also has a place in consumer-focused apps—duplicating a slide in a presentation tool, then editing the contents, is a well-used pattern.

Learning points

- Allow users to create a copy of an existing item in the system

- Don't force them to re-enter the same details every time

- Consider how this pattern can be applied to consumer products too

#81

MAKE IT EASY FOR USERS TO PAY YOU

The routes by which products are paid for are many and varied, but there is often the need for a product to ask a user to upgrade and enter some payment details.

Time and again, these interactions fall short of top-quality usability. Be they complex credit card forms, asking for too much information on lengthy order forms, or unclear pricing plan details, it's a massive missed opportunity.

To some extent, this is a solved problem in mobile apps—both iOS and Android include extensive support for in-app purchases and subscriptions. The user likely has their payment details saved and it's often a one-tap action to make a purchase.

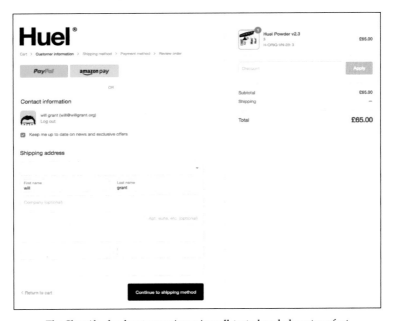

The Shopify checkout experience is well-tested and almost perfect

Out on the web, however, it's a different story. Although popular online stores like Shopify have helped to standardize this to some extent, it's often far too confusing and over-complicated in many products.

First up, there's pricing pages. Many pricing pages make it hard for the user to understand the various plans, subscriptions and add-on bundles. That's if the site even *has* a pricing page. Try to apply general UX principles to pricing pages:

- Overly long lists of features and benefits are hard to parse in the user's mind, so keep them short

- Make the "buy" button obvious with visual affordances

- Don't reinvent a weird and wonderful pricing structure—users spend the majority of their time on other products, not yours, so give users what they are familiar with

Basically, the principles in the rest of this book should be applied in particular to pricing pages.

Next, let's look at order forms. Make them simple, don't ask for unnecessary information, and give the user control over what they're buying (the ability to edit quantities and fine-tune their order).

Finally, make your payment form usable (there are principles on this elsewhere in this book). The user flow of learning about pricing, ordering a product or service, and paying, should be treated as one of your most important features. It's essential to your commercial survival.

Your user loves your product so much that they want to pay you, so make it as easy as possible and test this flow regularly.

Learning points

- Make payment and ordering pages as easy to use as possible
- Don't hide your pricing page away, and make it simple and clear
- Test your payment flow regularly

#82

CATEGORIZE SEARCH RESULTS INTO SECTIONS

Google is so *good* at ranking search results that users have come to expect this level of quality from all their search experiences. Unfortunately, the "out-of-the-box" site search on many modern web platforms is a little lacking. You will need to work hard on your product, and consider the whole search experience deeply, to deliver the kind of quality your users expect.

Don't return all the search results for a term in one huge list:

Cat spoon

Cat bed

Cat t-shirt

Cat food 500g

Cat food 1kg

Instead, split the results into sections—shorter lists help users to parse information more quickly, and they can skip to the section that's relevant to them:

Pet supplies (3)	Apparel (1)	Homeware (1)
Cat food 500g	Cat t-shirt	Cat spoon
Cat food 1kg		
Cat bed		

Show the user the number of items in each list, so they can decide whether clicking through to an especially long list is worth their time. As well as the benefit of saving your user time scanning the list, the categorization of results allows the user to filter by category, skipping straight to the most relevant section.

Split those search results up!

Learning points:

- Split search results into relevant categories
- Show the number of results in each category
- Aim to offer the user the same search quality they're used to elsewhere

#83

YOUR USERS PROBABLY
DON'T UNDERSTAND
THE FILE SYSTEM

The file system of your computer is the complex tree of many, many thousands of folders and files that make up the operating system—all your apps and their resources, and all your documents, images, and music files. Your users likely don't understand this—nor should they have to.

I've witnessed multiple people, in user tests, who use Microsoft Word as the primary way to find and retrieve information from their computer or network. They'll open Word and use the "open" command as a way to browse around their documents. If they come across an image, they'll open it into a Word document. If they want to send the image, they'll email a Word document with the image in. This probably sounds insane to most computer-literate people.

Of course, this makes perfect sense to users who mostly write and manage Word documents. They don't have any concept of the computer's file system, nor should they need to. These people aren't stupid— they just don't understand how files are stored on their computer.

When the iPad (and later, all tablets) rose to dominance as the "computer for people who don't need a computer," that was in part because of the fact that it obfuscated the file system from the user. On an iPad, there was no way to see the files: you had apps and documents within those apps. There was no way to accidentally delete an important system file and break the iPad.

In later releases, we have iCloud storage, which does complicate things a little, but the overall principle still holds. Open an app and your documents for that app are in there. There's no overall file system and this is a huge win for usability.

The point of this principle is to ask you to think about users' mental models of your products and how you store their information. When a user approaches your product fresh, they have to form a mental model of how it saves and retrieves their information. Does it save their files in the app? Do they need to download their work? If they start a task on their phone, can they continue it on their desktop? Make this clear to people.

There's no hard-and-fast rule for achieving this, save for following the other 100 principles in this book.

Learning points

- Users don't and shouldn't have to understand the file system of their device
- Make it clear to users how and where their work is saved
- Use this principle to consider what complexity you can helpfully hide from your users to improve their experience

#84

SHOW, DON'T TELL

The expression "show, don't tell" comes from screenwriting and fiction. Often attributed to playwright Anton Chekhov, the technique is intended to allow the reader to experience the story through action, words, senses and feelings, rather than through the author's exposition and description.

Show the viewer (or user) the situation and let them work out how they feel. It's also a great mantra to repeat to yourself if you're working on the experience of onboarding, feature guides, or other tuition—*showing* users how to use your product is always better than *telling* them.

The first reason for this is that *users don't read text.* Really, they don't. Time and again, in user test after user test, I've witnessed this with my own eyes—users simply don't read onscreen text. You have to show them how to use the product, not write a description using words.

Onscreen tips are a good starting point. The tips should be easily dismissible for repeat users (perhaps this isn't their first installation of this app), but present for new users. These tips can highlight areas of the app that allow the user to get started. Once they've been shown the key areas of the interface, you can leave them alone to discover more for themselves.

A video demo is best used for more complicated or highly specialized products. It's more intrusive and laborious to sit through, so please allow your veteran returning users to skip it. The benefits, of course, are more detailed and specific instructions on how to operate more complicated UI. This technique is used to great effect in professional software like video editors, graphics tools, and music software. Consumer products shouldn't need this.

A final way to make your "show, don't tell" approach more effective is to build upon established products (see *#95, Build Upon Established Metaphors – It's Not Stealing*). The chances are that your user has seen and experienced products like yours, so they can apply this experience to your product and be off to a flying start in no time.

Learning points

- Users seldom read text, so show them what you mean
- Video demos are great for complex software and UI
- Allow returning users to skip these demos

#85

BE CONSISTENT
WITH TERMINOLOGY

The words (or copy) that you write in your product have a dual purpose. The first is the most obvious: they label items and views and tell the user which elements are which.

The second is less obvious, but more important: the words you use become a very precise and descriptive *language* for your product. Understanding and parsing this language is essential to a user forming a mental model of how your product works.

If you call your e-commerce shopping cart a "cart", then call it "cart" *everywhere*.

If you call your user's profile page "profile", then call it "profile" *everywhere*.

If you call your user's email settings "email settings", then call them "email settings" *everywhere*.

Mix these up and it will take your user longer to ponder the inconsistent terms and work out what you mean.

Learning points:

- Use consistent terms across your product
- Don't just label things as you go—build a consistent language for your product
- Help users to form a mental model more quickly with consistent copy

#86

USE "SIGN IN"
AND "SIGN OUT",
NOT "LOG IN"
AND "LOG OUT"

Everyone has signed in to attend a meeting or visit a doctor or dentist. Signing in is something that people do in the real world. Nobody alive today has ever "logged in" in the real world. The term comes from the ship's log, where the sailor would log in their times and the distance travelled that day. It's highly unlikely that your users are 18th century seafarers!

Despite this, it's pretty common to see "log on" (or even worse: "logon") in software, and especially in business-to-business software that's been designed by developers.

For reasons of familiarity, always use "sign in" and "sign out" in your product consistently: they relate back to the real world. Unless your product is a mobile app for time-travelling pirates, of course.

Learning points

- Use "sign in" and "sign out" in your product
- Relate tasks like this to real-world situations for familiarity
- In particular, try to avoid the dreaded "logon"

#87

"SIGN UP" MAKES MORE SENSE THAN "REGISTER"

"Sign up" and "join" feel more human and friendly than "register", which, to me, feels like something the user is being forced to do. Most of the time, the user doesn't want to sign up to yet another product— it's a frustrating extra step, another password to remember and another load of emails that they're going to receive.

Of course, there are a lot of reasons why the user *needs* to make an account, but don't call it "register": it feels unfriendly and "sign up" goes hand in hand with "sign in", which I recommend instead of "log in" (see *#86, Use "Sign in" and "Sign out", Not "Log in" and "Log out"*).

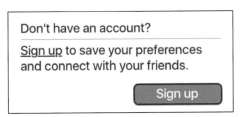

Friendly copy and clear control terms make this example highly usable

Combining the **Sign up** control with some well-written messaging can really help the app to feel more friendly and useful. In the preceding example, we're recapping the benefits of creating an account to inform a user *why* they may want to sign up.

Learning points

- Use "sign up" or "join" instead of "register"
- Tell the user the benefits of creating an account
- Be consistent across in-app copy and control labels

#88

USE "FORGOT PASSWORD" OR "FORGOTTEN YOUR PASSWORD", NOT SOMETHING OBSCURE

Password resets are a frequently-used part of the sign-in experience. Users will make mistakes and, as UX professionals, it's our job to help them out as best we can.

When it comes to passwords, unless you're using a password manager, you've:

- Got a password that's way too easy to remember and guess, or

- Forgotten your password

Allowing users to reset their password with an email or text message is a useful pattern, and it's so well-known that it should be standardized by now.

Even so, there are plenty of examples around the web and in mobile apps where unusual terminology or UI makes it unnecessarily hard to reset a password and get back into your account.

Call the control "forgot password" and not "reset your password", "can't access your account?", or "get a reset link." Most users won't necessarily understand that this is the route for their most common use case: they've forgotten their password.

If they've already entered their email address or username, pre-fill the "forgot password" form with that email or username—don't make them enter it all over again.

They should get (in their email or by SMS) a link that:

- Takes them to a page to set a new password
- Doesn't expire after one click (users double-click things frequently!)
- Does expire after a sensible time period
- Expires when the password has been successfully reset

Finally, consider allowing longer-lived sessions on your product. Despite some advice, *not* signing people out after a short period of time can actually *improve* security.

Once the user has signed in, their cookie or session token is stored securely in the browser or mobile device. If the device is lost or stolen, they likely have a PIN code or password on the device.

Automatically signing people out after a short time (30 minutes for an "enterprise app" or a couple of days for a mobile app) is bad: it means the user has to sign in more frequently.

This repeated signing in creates more hassle for them, a poorer experience and, as a result, they choose an easier password, making their account *less* secure.

Learning points

- Use "forgotten password" so the user knows that this is the function to solve that problem

- If the user has already entered their username, pre-fill it and don't ask for it again

- Consider allowing longer-lived sign-in sessions on your product

#89

WRITE LIKE
A HUMAN BEING

Too often, terminology in software is written from a systems-oriented or organization-centric point of view. We often see menu options like "edit customer" or "create new customer", but stop and think about this for a second—customers are people and we don't create them. The first option doesn't actually *edit a customer* and the second doesn't *create a new customer*.

For the developer, customers are just database records, so of course it makes sense to edit them and create new ones, but for the user, these options should be better named: "edit a customer's details" and "add a new customer".

This principle is best achieved through objectivity and empathy. In other words, being able to step outside of your view of a product and see it through a customer's eyes. You must take this step to build usable software and it's worth the effort.

The words that you use for in-product copy, for menu controls and even for marketing materials, have power and weight: you can use them to welcome or alienate people, to set them on the right path or to confuse and bewilder them. Put effort into your writing and you'll build products that people love to use.

Learning points

- Write from a user-centric not an organization-centric point of view
- Don't let "corporate speak" creep into your product
- Consider how the words you use can affect people's perceptions of your product

#90

CHOOSE ACTIVE VERBS OVER PASSIVE

Most of this book is concerned with using visual design to improve the user's experience. However, the *words* that we use as designers also have a huge impact on the usability of the products we create.

10 years ago, I found myself on a half-day course by the Plain English Campaign (the body behind the "Crystal Mark" for documents that are easy to read and understand). There were a lot of great tips on the course, but the section on the active and passive voice really stuck with me:

> **"A verb is in the passive voice when the subject of the sentence is acted on by the verb. For example, in 'the ball was thrown by the pitcher', the ball (the subject) receives the action of the verb, and 'was thrown' is in the passive voice. The same sentence cast in the active voice would be, 'The pitcher threw the ball.'"** – **Dictionary.com (Definition of the** active **(https://www.dictionary.com/browse/active-voice) and** passive **(http://www.dictionary.com/browse/passive-voice) voice)**

Now, because the active voice is more direct, it requires fewer mental steps for the user to "unpack" the meaning. In UX, this translates into interfaces that can be used and understood faster.

Switching your copy to the active voice can make it sound less stuffy and bureaucratic—and users will appreciate this simplicity. Consider the following sentences:

- This matter will be considered by us shortly (passive verb)

- We will consider this matter shortly (active verb)

The active voice is crisper and uses fewer words. When applied to the field of software design, we can make on screen copy much easier to read. The following are some examples:

- "In order to apply updates, your computer must be restarted" is passive. Compare that to the clearer and more punchy "please restart your computer to apply updates".

- "The "search" button should be clicked once you have entered search terms" could be replaced with the much simpler "enter search terms and click "search"."

It's possibly because most software is designed within large, bureaucratic organizations that this language creeps in over time. The passive voice is often associated with sounding more officious or formal, when in reality it just sounds pompous and confusing.

As products evolve, more and more stakeholders inevitably weigh in to have their say: branding want the copy to reflect the brand values, legal want it to be factually accurate and watertight, the growth hackers want to stuff keywords in, and so on. What users are then presented with is a watered-down, passive version of the original idea, which is overly complex and indirect.

The passive voice makes your interfaces slower to use and harder to understand, so root it out and destroy it.

Learning points

- Choose the active voice over the passive voice for in-app copy
- Continually review your copy and labels to ensure they still make sense
- Test phrases on real users and work out which get the best results

#91

SEARCH RESULTS
PAGES SHOULD
SHOW THE MOST
RELEVANT RESULT AT
THE TOP OF THE PAGE

Of all the principles in this guide, this might be the number one no-brainer. Of *course*, show the user the most relevant results first. Yet, time and again, this principle is broken and users are shown irrelevant items first in their results.

So, why have you asked the user to search, then shown them a poor set of results?

Reason 1: your search algorithm sucks.

Technically, this is the toughest one to solve. Ranking search results is, in some cases, a tricky technical problem, but there are tried and tested technologies (TF-IDF is a very popular algorithm for ranking text documents: see `term frequency-inverse document frequency` (https://en.wikipedia.org/wiki/Tf%E2%80%93idf)) and a lot of off-the-shelf search tools will include some sensible defaults.

It's a difficult task to make your search perform as well as Google's search does—but that's what users expect. Users don't understand that 1,000 person-years of effort has gone into Google's ranking algorithm: they expect your site to rank results just as effectively (see *#82, Categorize Search Results into Sections*).

Test searches, pore over your site analytics, see what the most popular search terms are and make damn sure that those results are relevant.

Reason 2: your filter defaults are bad.

Maybe your results are coming back from the database in a decent ranking, but you're applying some poorly-chosen filters to them. For example, if a user is searching an auction site for items, only to be shown the closest first. It might have seemed like a good idea—because you have the user's location—but if they're getting the item shipped, then it's not relevant and there may be a better, cheaper item further down the list. Pick sensible defaults and show the user which ones you've picked, allowing them to change them at will (see *#92, Pick Good Defaults*).

Reason 3: you're trying to sell the user something that they don't want.

A more sinister reason is that many sites will show you the items *they want you to see*, rather than the items that you want to see. This serves nothing but the internal needs of the organization. It's a surefire way to enrage users, so don't do it. You might sell a few more car rentals, but at the expense of pissing off most of your customers.

Learning points

- Show users the most relevant results at the top of a search results page
- Give users clear controls to modify the results with sort order and filters
- Think like your users—what results would it be *best for your users* to see first?

#92

PICK GOOD DEFAULTS

The power of default settings is often overlooked, but they have huge potential to affect the UX of your product.

Some examples of great defaults:

- When I get into my car, the default sound output of my phone switches from handset to in-car speaker. I can change it, but the default is sensible.

- Sign in to an analytics product and the selected date range is "this week", with a comparison date range of "last week." Imagine if the default was "today" and showed no data—useless, right?

- When I tap a name in my "recent calls" view, my phone calls that person, rather than starting a new text message or video call. Those options are tucked away in a context menu.

Picking a good default is a balance of factors:

- How many users you think (or know through research) want *this* default setting

- How difficult it is for the user to change to an alternative

- How discoverable that alternative setting is

As a UX professional, it's your job to weigh up these factors and a lot of that judgement will be based on "gut feeling", as well as evidence.

There's a temptation to expose a new feature or functionality—just because it's new—and make it the default setting. Don't do this. Your users don't care about something because it's new: they care whether it's useful or not.

How many times have you heard users complain, "They've updated the app and now it makes you do X"? If X was an option, rather than the new default, you'd have happier users.

A final thought—be aware that the vast majority of users don't venture into settings menus and will simply use a product with its default setup. For the bulk of your users, the default setting is the *only* setting, so choose well.

Learning points

- Think carefully about the default settings you choose
- Most users will never change from the defaults
- Balance the factors of discoverability and frequency of use when deciding on defaults

#93

DON'T CONFOUND USERS' EXPECTATIONS

This is a kind of meta-principle. When your customers approach your product, they bring with them a lot of baggage. This past experience can be fought against or worked with. It's your job to work with it.

Consider that your users have almost certainly:

- Used a computer or a smartphone before
- Used a web-based product or an app before
- Used a product a bit like yours before
- Used a product "very much" like yours before

  So why make things hard for them?

Your users have spent *many years* using products *just like yours*, so should your product work *just like* those other products or radically differently?

The answer is—"just like those other products".

iOS, Android and Tizen. There's a reason that products look similar

It's not exciting or sexy—you're not inventing a whole new class of product or interface, and you're not revolutionizing a whole product sector. What you are doing is the good work of a UX professional: building on the established practices that users know and love from years of experience.

Your satisfaction comes not from reinventing the wheel but from giving the user a wheel that they already know how to use. This will give them the tools to get their jobs done and improve their life just a little bit.

Learning points

- Users bring their past experience of other products with them to your product
- Make your product work like other products your users have experienced
- Don't reinvent the wheel

#94

REDUCE THE NUMBER
OF TASKS A USER
HAS TO COMPLETE
BY USING SENSIBLE
DEFAULTS

A big benefit of thinking through your default settings (see *#92, Pick Good Defaults*) is that a good set of defaults can radically reduce the number of tasks that a user has to perform.

Consider a shopping site where the user searches for "pyjamas for kids." The search results shown to the user have already selected a series of defaults in the left-hand filter panel:

- Category: children's clothing
- Age: 2 to 15
- In stock

Without these intelligent defaults, the user would have to search for the relevant controls and configure them. It would only be a few extra clicks, but these tasks take time.

Through the use of user testing, A/B testing and analytics research, it should be possible to identify common user journeys and optimize the defaults for the vast majority of users.

These kinds of studies often yield results that follow the "80/20 rule" or Pareto principle (read more about the Pareto principle on Wikipedia (https://en.wikipedia.org/wiki/Pareto_principle)): optimizing the top 20% of user journeys can have a positive impact on 80% of your users.

Learning points

- Using sensible defaults can reduce the effort users have to put in
- Combine insights from user testing, A/B testing, and analytics research
- Usually, a little effort in a few product areas goes a long way towards improving your product's default settings

#95

BUILD UPON ESTABLISHED METAPHORS – IT'S NOT STEALING

Over the years, I've found that part of the imagined "code of practice" of designers is to not steal. As we train and learn, we're taught to develop our own design style and not to borrow too much. Imitation is discouraged and copying the designs of others is frowned upon, dishonest even.

In UX, this is the polar opposite of best practice. Consider `Jakob's Law of Internet User Experience` (https://www.nngroup.com/videos/ jakobs-law-internet-ux/), which states, "Users spend most of their time on other sites. This means that users prefer your site to work the same way as all the other sites they already know".

Jakob Nielsen utterly nails it with this one. Your users spend the vast majority of their lives *not using your product*. They spend that time on other sites, other web apps and other mobile apps. The product with which they're *least familiar* is *your* product.

You should aim to build upon established patterns:

- Forms that allow simple data entry, easy movement between fields, and a "submit" or "save" button

- Toggle controls that adjust a setting to be either on or off

- Pages or views in your product that tell users how much the product costs, in total, without hidden fees

- Obvious controls, links that look like links and buttons that resemble buttons

- Search that works quickly and shows the most relevant items first

Much of this book, although based on practice and real-world experience, focuses on collecting and distilling the best practices of *what's already out there.* Make your product like all the other products your customer already knows how to use.

Learning points

- Don't be shy about borrowing best practices from other products

- Users want your product to work like products they already know and use

- Build upon established patterns to achieve this

#96

DECIDE WHETHER AN INTERACTION SHOULD BE OBVIOUS, EASY, OR POSSIBLE

While we strive to make our products as intuitive and familiar as possible, there will always be "advanced" options and rarely-used features (see *#26, Hide "Advanced" Settings From Most Users*). Giving users choice and control over their experience will naturally lead to features that are used less frequently or settings that only a small percentage of users will change.

To help decide where (and how prominently) a control or interaction should be placed, it's useful to classify interactions into one of three types:

- **Obvious:** Obvious interactions are the core function of the app, for example, the shutter button on a camera app or the new event button on a calendar app. They're the functions that users will likely perform every time they use your product and their controls should be visible and intuitive. Hiding these away—either accidentally or intentionally—does still happen and it's often a cause of massive frustration for users and the failure of new products.

- **Easy**: Easy interactions are the hardest to classify and often we'll only get these right after several rounds of iteration and user feedback. For example, an easy interaction could be switching between the front-facing and rear-facing lens in a camera app, or editing an existing event in a calendar app. The controls should be easily found, perhaps in a menu or as a secondary-level item in the main controls. They're the toughest to get right because they're used too frequently to be tucked away, but they are not used every time, which means designers will often de-prioritize them too heavily.

- **Possible**: Interactions we classify as possible are rarely used and they are often advanced features. They need to be discoverable, but they shouldn't be given the same prominence as obvious or easy interactions. For example, it is possible to adjust the white balance or auto-focus on a camera app, or make an event recurring on a calendar app. These advanced controls can be tucked further away, as the majority of users will not need to see their UI cluttered with them.

The iOS camera UI balances these three classes of interaction well

These decisions are vital to the success of your UI and therefore the UX and product as a whole. Start early—at the paper prototyping or wireframe stage. Test often—looking at what users are doing and how they are discovering features and settings. Iterate quickly—make changes and get them shipped and tested as fast as you can. Only then will you get the balance between obvious, easy and possible correct for your product and your users.

Learning points

- Decide whether interactions should be obvious, easy, or possible
- Test your assumptions with real users
- Iterate quickly in the early stages of your products to ensure success

#97

"DOES IT WORK
ON MOBILE?"
IS OBSOLETE

It feels like the terms "mobile-first", "Mobile-friendly" and "responsive design" have stopped being worth mentioning—they are a given. Everything is now assumed to be responsive and mobile-first, and it's considered a breaking bug if your web app doesn't work on mobile, not to mention it being a death sentence for your SEO.

Modern frontend frameworks make it simple to build a web app or site that responds to different viewports, makes controls the right size for mobile and "gracefully degrades" (hiding elements that don't work on smaller devices). Responsive design means that the UI will adapt to different device sizes automatically, so you don't have to build a distinct "mobile version" of your product.

What's more, web apps are often better for the user than native mobile apps. This isn't a strict rule, as there are lots of reasons why you might need a native app—access to device features or heavy-duty computation or logic—but always consider whether a web app might be a better choice. Web apps need no installation, don't have to be submitted to an app store, work across any platform with a web browser, and can be updated instantly without a download.

Also consider that a mobile-first approach helps you to reduce and simplify the experience in the design phase. I've watched users, in user testing, opt to use the mobile version of the site because it's cleaner and simpler.

Learning points

- Your software has to work on mobile—it's no longer optional
- Modern front end frameworks make this easy to achieve
- Starting from a mobile-first position can help the overall design process

#98

MESSAGING IS A SOLVED PROBLEM

Messaging has been done so many times and has been perfected to the point that the patterns are well-established. Yet, we still see products that have decided to reinvent the wheel or implement their own weird take on the messaging feature, causing confusion and user frustration aplenty.

Here's how it should work:

- The messaging feature should show the number of unread messages

- Using the messaging feature should show an "inbox", which contains a list of messages grouped by recipient and sorted by date last contacted

- The inbox list should, if possible, show an extract from the last message sent in that thread

- Viewing an item (a recipient) should show a list of all messages sent and received, with the latest messages first

- Viewing an item should "clear" the unread notification and reduce the total number of unread items

- There should be a text area or text input field with the message thread that sends a reply to that recipient

- The message area should support new lines, so hitting "return" doesn't send a half-finished message

These tips are simple, but effective and well-practiced. Please don't confuse your users with your radical, innovative take on what should be a very simple and established pattern.

Learning points

- Don't reinvent the wheel on messaging features
- Borrow from the well-established patterns already in widespread use
- Don't send the message with "return" before it's fini—

#99

BRANDS ARE BULLSHIT

I don't mean brand in the sense of visual identity—a good logo, wordmark or tagline is a great idea. I mean brand in the modern sense—a woolly definition that's come to be commonplace over the past 10 years or so.

The word brand has come to allude to the company or to stand for the entire personality of a corporation or product. It is seen as the "feeling" of interacting with products and services, and inevitably the core interactions of those products.

The problem with this approach, developed for over a decade by multinational branding corporations, is that *we already have a discipline for this: UX*. By crafting a product to adhere to a brand (in the modern sense of the word), we defer control of the UX to the marketing and branding teams, not the UX professionals.

I'm not talking about the megabrands with a billion customers; Apple, Google, Coca-Cola, Microsoft, Nike, and so on are so big and their brands so powerful that it *does* and *should* make a difference to how their products are designed.

What about your brand, with a few thousand or tens of thousands of customers, or your small company, product, or newly-launched start-up? *Nobody cares*. Harsh, but true. None of your users care about your brand. They care about what your product or service *lets them do*. They care about how your product improves their lives and enhances their productivity, and so on.

The experience of your product *is* your brand and it shouldn't be designed by a marketing team, but by UX people. This is also your competitive advantage against the big, lumbering dinosaurs that have to adhere rigidly to brand guides.

Don't let the brand guide ruin your product with:

- **Unreadable brand typefaces**: Just use the native system font stack

- **Branded splash screens**: Just show me the damn app

- **Build-your-own nightmarish UI controls**: Oh, the things I've seen...

- **Awful, unreadable contrast ratios**: Don't stick to the brand palette if it doesn't work in your product

- **Unnecessarily quirky copy**: The "wacky" humor on the side of a smoothie bottle

A brand can help to enforce consistency, but, if you're a decent designer, you shouldn't need a brand guide to tell you how to build consistent UI. Brands are bullshit, so focus on the UX and the experience *becomes* the brand.

Learning points

- Nobody cares about your brand, only about what your product lets them do
- A good UX is better than a good brand
- Fight for the user, not the brand guide

#100

DON'T JOIN
THE DARK SIDE

People check their smartphones a *lot*. One reason for this is that, in some way, it's a gamble. You check your phone and maybe there are no notifications or maybe there's a "red blob." Maybe someone's "liked" your Facebook post or someone's "faved" your Instagram picture of your brunch or your pet.

Each time you get a notification, you feel happy—your brain releases a little bit of dopamine. So, you wait a little while and you check your phone again, hoping for the same result and reinforcing the addictive behavior loop.

This isn't an accident. Many modern products, especially social media, are *designed* to be addictive. In Hooked—A Guide to Building Habit-Forming Products, Portfolio Penguin, 2014 (https:// amzn.to/2pItKo0), psychologist *Nir Eyal* proposes the Hook Model: "A four-step process that, when embedded into products, subtly encourages customer behavior.

Through consecutive 'hook cycles,' these products bring people back again and again without depending on costly advertising or aggressive messaging."

In order to *not* send your contacts to Facebook, you need to tap "Learn More."

Next, there's so-called "dark patterns", which are UI or UX patterns designed to *trick* the user into doing what the corporation or brand wants them to do. These are, in a way, exactly the same as the scams used by old-time fraudsters and rogue traders, now transplanted to the web and updated for the post-internet age. You'll definitely have come across some of these:

- Shopping carts that add extra "add-on" items (like insurance, protection policies, and so on) to your cart before you check out, hoping that you won't remove them

- Search results that begin their list by showing the item *they'd like to sell you* instead of the best result

- Ads that don't look like ads, so you accidentally tap them

- Changing a user's settings—edit your private profile and if you don't explicitly make it private again, the company will switch it back to public

- Unsubscribe "confirmation screens", where you have to uncheck a ton of checkboxes *just right* to actually unsubscribe

- Software in an automobile engine management computer that checks whether the vehicle is being emissions tested and, if so, lowers the performance and emissions

I could go on—there are hundreds. Please don't do any of them.

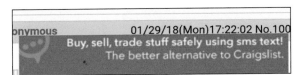

This mobile banner ad has a "speck of dirt" on the image, in the hope that the user will accidentally tap when they try to remove it

In some fields, medicine for example, professionals have a code of conduct and ethics that forms the core of the work they do. Building software does not have such a code of conduct, but maybe it should do.

All of these dark patterns and addictive products were designed by normal people working in normal software companies—they had a choice. They chose to fight for the company, not the user. Be a good UX professional and don't join the dark side.

Learning points

- Think about the moral and ethical implications of the software you help to create
- Design interfaces and experiences that you'd want to use
- Fight for the user, not the company

#101

TEST WITH REAL USERS

This principle is presented last in the list deliberately, to emphasize its importance. Nothing in this book means anything unless you test with real people.

You need to test with real users, not your colleagues, not your boss and not your partner. You need to test with a diverse mix of people, from the widest section of society you can get access to.

User testing is an essential step to understanding not just your product, but the users you're testing— what their goals really are, how they want to achieve them, and where your product delivers or falls short. You'll not only understand your users better, but you'll reduce development time by short-circuiting the feedback loop and getting problems fixed much earlier in the product life cycle.

It's never too early to start testing—an unfinished prototype or even paper prototype (cards or post-it notes that you move around on a desk) can yield valuable insights—so get your product in front of users as soon as you can.

So, what are you testing? User tests are, in themselves, a broad spectrum of activities ranging from "guerilla-style" tests—where you approach a random person and ask them to perform a task in the app—through to specific feature-based tests, where an expert user (usually with domain knowledge) is asked to perform a complex task. Either way, you need to start with an idea of what you're testing, tuned to both the complexity level of the product and the domain knowledge that a user needs to operate it.

There's a myth that user testing is expensive and time-consuming, but the reality is that even very small test groups (fewer than 10 people) can provide fascinating insights. The nature of such tests is very qualitative and doesn't lend itself well to quantitative analysis, so you can learn a lot from working with a small sample set of fewer than 10 users.

There's research (*Why you only need to test with 5 users*, NNG (https://www.nngroup.com/articles/why-you-only-need-to-test-with-5-users/)) to show that testing with as few as five users will uncover 85% of usability problems in a single test. This startlingly high number is found thanks to the Poisson distribution and some math.

Too often, products aren't tested, the thinking being that "we'll just hear what users don't like and fix it." The problem is *your users won't tell you*; they'll just leave. The near-infinite choice of products and services on the web, app stores and a myriad of devices means that the user has no incentive to stay, complain, and help you to improve your product—it will simply fail.

Test with real users and listen to them, and you'll build something they love.

Learning points

- Test your product early and with real users
- Test with a mix of ages and genders
- You only need to test with a small group to get huge benefits

BONUS – STRIVE
FOR SIMPLICITY

> **"A designer knows he has achieved perfection not when there is nothing left to add, but when there is nothing left to take away."**

—Antoine de Saint-Exupéry

Strive for simplicity and clarity in every aspect of your work. Not just in the interfaces, copy and experiences you design, but in the words you say in meetings and in the emails you write.

Avoid jargon, put people at ease and try to improve the UX of everyone you interact with.

Your mock-ups and wireframes should be simple and usable, but so should all other aspects of you – the product.

Make yourself a delight for others to interact with.

OTHER BOOKS
YOU MAY ENJOY

If you enjoyed this book, you may be interested in these other books by Packt:

Hands-On UX Design for Developers

Elvis Canziba

ISBN: 978-1-78862-669-9

- What UX is and what a UX designer does
- Explore the UX Process and science of making products user-friendly
- Create user interfaces and learn which tools to use
- Understand how your design works in the real world
- Create UI interaction, animation, wireframes, and prototypes
- Design a product with users in mind
- Develop a personal portfolio and be well-prepared to join the UX world

Fixing Bad UX Designs

Lisandra Maioli

ISBN: 978-1-78712-055-6

- Learn about ROI and metrics in UX

- Understand the importance of getting stakeholders involved

- Learn through real cases how to fix bad UX

- Identify and fix UX issues using different methodologies

- Learn how to turn insights and finding into practical UX solutions

- Learn to validate, test and measure the UX solutions implemented

- Learn about UX refactoring

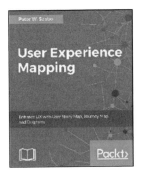

User Experience Mapping

Peter W. Szabo

ISBN: 978-1-78712-350-2

- Create and understand all common user experience map types.

- Use lab or remote user research to create maps and understand users better.

- Design behavioral change and represent it visually.

- Create 4D user experience maps, the "ultimate UX deliverable".

- Capture many levels of interaction in a holistic view.

- Use experience mapping in an agile team, and learn how maps help in communicating within the team and with stakeholders.

- Become more user focused and help your organization become user-centric.

Leave a review - let other readers know what you think

Please share your thoughts on this book with others by leaving a review on the site that you bought it from. If you purchased the book from Amazon, please leave us an honest review on this book's Amazon page. This is vital so that other potential readers can see and use your unbiased opinion to make purchasing decisions, we can understand what our customers think about our products, and our authors can see your feedback on the title that they have worked with Packt to create. It will only take a few minutes of your time, but is valuable to other potential customers, our authors, and Packt. Thank you!

INDEX

A

active voice
selecting, over passive
voice 334-336
advanced settings
hiding 92-94
animated progress bar 212
animated spinner 208
arbitrary controls 32

B

blank slate 68, 70
body copy 16
breadcrumb navigation
using 272, 273
buttons
about 22-24
clickable 30
creating 26, 27

C

card details
collecting 190, 191
case-insensitive 156
color indicators
creating 240, 241
contrast ratio 218
create from existing flow
adding 300
create from existing option
adding 301
**CRUD (Stands for create, read,
update, and delete)**
currency input 198

D

data entry
validating 166, 167
date picker
using 148, 149

default settings
about 342, 343
using 350, 351
descriptive links
using 232, 233
design patterns, hamburger menu
navigation on the bottom of the
view 81
tabbed navigation 81
vertical type 81
**device-native input
controls 122, 123**
drop-downs 48, 186-187

E

eCommerce pattern
about 284, 285
basket 285
checkout 285
products 284
edges of items
displaying 54, 55
ellipsis
using 18, 19
email addresses
validation, avoiding on client
side 134, 135
Emoji
using 118, 119
established patterns
building 354, 355

F

Favicon
creating 296, 297
feed
refreshing 76
field labels
writing 252, 253
file system 312, 313
Flash of unstyled content (FOUC)
about 8
reference link 8

H

I

L

M

N

O

P

R

S

T

tab key
adding, to navigate 248
terminology
consistency 320
test application
using 291
text
avoiding, in icons 110, 111
text field
with button labeled search 36, 37
text label
displaying, with icons 114, 115
Tweetie 32
typefaces 6
type size
using 13, 14

U

UI control
about 144, 145, 178, 179, 280, 281
autosaving 288
data, entering 174, 175
designing 260, 261
forgotten password, using 326, 327
orders, creating 304-306
payment form, using 304-306
sign in, using 322
sign out, using 322
sign up, using instead register 324
undo destructive actions 50, 51
user controls
about 268, 269
skip button, adding to 276, 277
user-entered data 138
user interface (UI)
about 23, 264, 266 370, 371
designing 374-377
phone number, detecting 183, 184

username
pre-filling, on forgot password
field 152, 153
user's position 66
user testing 380, 381
UX professional 2, 3

V

Vanity Splash Screen
avoiding 294
visual affordances
used, on controls 222-224

W

**Web Content Accessibility
Guidelines (WCAG) 218**
Wide Web Consortium (W3C) 218

Made in the USA
Lexington, KY
02 January 2019